SAIL THE STORM

SAILING A STORM IS NEVER EASY, BUT DEFINITELY NOT IMPOSSIBLE

DANIEL ABHISHIKTH B

Contents

Preface

A very large number of people dream big in their lives, but very few people decide to make their dreams come true. I'm one among them. All it takes is one strong decision for a completely new episode of life. Becoming successful in life is beyond Riches, Fame, and Freedom. It's more like becoming a completely different person through all the struggles and enlightenments in the journey or the sail to the big dreams.

A successful person is the improved version of his/her past self and personality. The way they see the world changes, and the way they respond to obstacles changes. Mindsets will be unimaginably changed, the way we think today is our tomorrow. I've realized the definition of being successful in the early stages of my sail to my dream. And as I have no mentors around me to take guidance from, I figured out how the mindset, character, and personality should be built to achieve the big dreams in life. So this made me write this book in which I have mentioned how we should build ourselves to achieve our goals. Becoming successful is being promoted from 98% of the population in the world to the top 2% of the population. It's all learning and improving, and success makes its way to us at some point in time. All of my research, experiences, lessons, proofs, examples, and concepts were included in this book. Hope this book brings the best out of you for yourself.

This book is worth reading for anyone who is building something big or has higher goals to achieve in their lives, this book could be a reference in many steps of achieving your dream. The concepts, stories, examples, research, inspirations, realities, motivations, and many which are all needed for a journey to the goals are in this book. Happy reading

Introduction

This book helps in all walks of life, especially when you are building something important and something big. It could be a business, a career in any unique stream, or an organization. Building something is hard. We need to experience every struggle, every trouble, then make mistakes and repeat no mistakes and keep on working without taking a break and not quitting. After a while or a long while you will achieve what you wanted.

This book doesn't tell you how to build your business or your career, But this book helps you in how to make your mind or train your mind while building something big or something important in life. The whole process of thinking should be in a different way when you are on a mission. Distractions and barriers should not divert the interest or make you lose hope. This book could make you sense the upcoming situations while building something for which you could be ready to face and pass by.

If building something takes 7 long Years individually, It would take 4 years with the help of mentors. Mentors are important because they are experienced and they know beforehand what problems are going to come and what should be the counter to win that phase. Mentors make the building process easy not only for Your career or business but also for your thinking process when you are doing something very important. A mentor could be a completely different person, or sometimes your father or an elderly person, or sometimes your boss or friend who walked through the same paths before. It could also be a book or an article. This book doesn't give

100% mentorship but guides a major part of the thinking process while building something or while running to achieve something great unlike a major population of people.

The journey to my storm started when I decided to be an entrepreneur with few ideas in my mind. I started building ideas and at the same time working night shifts on the vast floor of the corporate office when I'm 21 years old. My constant thought was how to convey my decision to my parents and how to convince them to accept my decision.

"To take this step in life, any individual needs a lot of Trust, Faith, Hope, Optimism, Talent, and capability".

The above-underlined sentence was my 1st mistake. I told myself I got all those which are mentioned above and more over got confidence too. And it didn't take a lot of time for me to realize that this is way harder, way more different, and way more complicated.

This book contains what I have not seen coming, what I learned, and how I made myself and stood up.

Sail The Storm

"Sailing a storm is never easy, but definitely not impossible"

The title says it all.

The title says it all, the explanation: Sail is survival and hard work in the title, the work, and efforts which you put to survive or to achieve something great imply 'Sail' in the title. Storm implies a whole of a journey to the dream, goal, business, Startup, Sport, or in any walk of life. When you know you belong to the 2% population of the world and started to build something big or started to achieve something great then here you go, you can't skip the storm. Achieving and winning your goal or target is not easy, and yes definitely not impossible. It is as simple as it is, Sail the storm and you win. Prepare yourself for the storm, accept the situation and be ready to work hard, consistently, and deal with each and everything that you don't see coming in the storm. A long and hard sail needs more than what you can ever imagine.

On November 17, 2012, A Salvadoran(country in central America) fisherman named Alvarenga set off on a professional fishing trip with a young fisherman named Ezequiel cordoba. With whom he had never worked. Having embarked from a fishing village on the pacific coast of Mexico's southern Chiapas state, they planned to be out about 30 hours hunting shark, tuna, and mahi-

mahi. A few hours into their voyage a storm struck that lasted 5 days and blew them off course. Alvarenga tried calling his boss on the ship's radio for help but the radio and much of the ship's electronics had been disabled by the storm. The boat's motor was also damaged.

A search party was sent, but after two days with no success, their boss gave up and assumed that they had drowned

As the fishermen were off for only a 30-hour trip there was no food stored. Alone and without food or supplies, the two fishermen survived by eating raw fish, turtles, and jellyfish. They drank rainwater and turtle blood. As weeks turned to months cordoba became severely unwell from eating months of raw food and died.

Alvarenga then endured another 9 months alone at sea. Until he eventually spotted a small island. Abandoning his boat and swam to shore. He almost immediately met a local couple who alerted authorities. He had reached the Marshall Islands.

His journey lasted 438 days and his voyage is estimated to have covered between 5500 to 6700 miles.

On the day he started on the trip with another fisherman he never worked with earlier he did not know what was coming. He was prepared only for a 30-hour fishing trip. But he very quickly saw a storm hitting him, then lost the connections, then hunger, thirst, and so many more which he never saw coming. To survive 438 days in which most of them are alone, his hard work, talent, capability, and faith are not all he should have. There are plenty of other characteristics involved which pulled him through. He accepted he had to have them to survive and none of those characteristics are similar to his daily routine in the normal world.

Sailing the storm is never said to be easy, it's tough, it is hard, every decision is at risk, and a lot of determination is needed. And yes it's not impossible. You can sail the storm when you are that kind of capable person who has the skill and desire to sail. Your dream or ambition could be a startup, Business, Education, sports, or any walk of life, when you are on a mission you will need to work on what you never worked on before to win that phase. Accept the situation and that is when you could genuinely realize what to act and then work on it. It's always tough in every phase of the mission and journey, but not impossible if you make yourself ready for all the struggles and learn from them and master them.

TRUST YOURSELF AS YOUR MOM DOES

"Trust is an illusion"

Belief in ideas or goals and Trust in ourselves is a completely different thing in sailing. It is not as simple as having a gut feeling called the belief that what I am working on will be a huge hit and having trust that I CAN DO IT. It's way more complicated to understand this concept, but once we do understand it, that's when we will know how hard it is to trust ourselves and have faith in what we are doing.

"Trusting ourselves and believing in our dream is the combination of Skill, Interest, and effort."

I went through a lot of thought processes to assign a title for this chapter and end up with "Trust yourself as your mom does". Why this title? My brother peeked into my desktop and questioned me. As a response, I asked him to call mom and ask her "Mom how do I look?" He did so, although he shouted so that mom who was in the kitchen could hear him. Mom replied You are pretty handsome, my son. That's a lovely reply, now I asked him to tell her "I'm planning to become an actor in movies as HERO because I'm handsome" then my mom walked into us, With a sarcastic expression on her face, said, ``Hero? You? Never mind. And she left.

This explains him a lot. It doesn't matter how handsome her son is to her, but there are lots of people more handsome than her son and also, apart from looks she still thinks he cannot become an actor because he needs more than looks, he needs skill, own interest, passion, talent and many more. So a mother's belief in her child is in this way, she believes in her children but that belief has got a point of realization (when it comes to career and life decisions). Mothers don't give false beliefs or forceful beliefs which will affect their children's future or careers. And if you say to your mom, Mom I want to become a musician or an actor or whatever and I want to take courses to learn, I have to work on it. I'm so passionate about that, it's my dream and then the way a mother responds is different. They encourage you towards your goal even though they feel your journey towards your dream is almost impossible they will still encourage you to give it a try. But it's different if you have no talent, no skill and you are rushing on a dream. No mother will let you waste your time over that. Moms trust their children in the learning process. They believe in what their children are working on, If they are trying hard to achieve something, learning and improving in their respective walk of the dream. They encourage you to learn, encourage you to work hard, encourage you to keep trying, and such processes.

There is a major difference between the words TRUST and BELIEF.

Don't confuse them, Trust: Firm belief in the reliability, truth, or ability of something or someone. When you already know the ability of a person and know he is capable of winning that phase just like in cricket a great batsman who got an amazing strike rate is at the crease and there is 1 over left and 20 runs to win you think he can still make it. That's when it is called trust. Belief: An acceptance that something exists or is true when there is no proof. This is strange, how can we trust something without proof. That's what belief is, it is so powerful when you believe correctly.

When you are sailing the storm, belief does come alone, It comes along with trust, Trust yourself, Believe in your Dream or idea or work

Trust yourself

Trusting yourself is never easy, if you find trusting yourself is easy in sailing then you must be a master at your work or a dumb. The term 'Trust yourself' means trusting your capabilities, talents, and interests to conquer your dream.

To trust yourself you need to completely know yourself. All your capabilities, strengths, weaknesses, Interests, every little quality, and mindset. And this process is hard because it should be genuine. To achieve your dream or goal or target, big or small tasks, know yourself in the first place, completely, genuinely. And then realize what characteristics you need to build, and what skills you need to work on. But when you are not able to be genuine with yourself and realize what exactly you are, and yet you think you trust yourself then that's an Illusion. This illusion of self-trust is the path to failure. If you just repeat saying I trust myself that I can jump over that ten feet barrier. No, You can't do it just by trusting yourself. You should be capable of doing it and that needs a lot of practice, and effort and you should be able to trust your capabilities.

So, if you know what you are and what you are trying for, when you know it's a tough road and how good you can drive, when you know which way the wind is blowing and how smart to sail, you can sail better. When you know your capabilities then you will learn, you will improve and you can withstand a million storms.

"The illusion of Self Trust is the path to failure"
-Jia Jiang

Jia Jiang grew up in Beijing, China. When he was six years old, one day in school all the students received gifts. His 1st-grade teacher had this brilliant idea(says Jiang), she wanted all the students to experience receiving gifts but also learning the virtue of complementing. So she asked all the students to come to the front of the classroom and she bought all of her gifts and stacked them in the corner she told everyone to stand here and complement each other if they hear their name called go and pick up your gifts and sit down. There were 40 students in his class and the process began, whenever Jiang heard someone's name called he gave out the heartiest cheer. The process is going pretty well and at last, there are only 3 students left and compliments stopped coming and Jia Jiang is one among those three 6-year-olds.

At that moment Jiang wept, he didn't want to receive any gift and listen to any compliments, he just wanted to get out of there and sit down. Then his teacher freaked out and said, Hey, would anyone see anything nice about these people, No? Okay. Go pick up your gifts and sit down and behave well from now on, so someone might say something nice about you next year. This rejection at age of 6 stuck in Jia Jiang's mind for years. He was so embarrassed and had a fear of rejection started in him.

Eight years from then Bill gates had been to Jia Jiang's home town Beijing, China to speak and Jiang was inspired a lot by bill gates and embraced his idea and conquering world domination. That night he wrote a letter to his family saying By age 25 I will build the biggest company in the world and that company will buy Microsoft. Two years later when he was 16 he migrated to the United States.

He wanted to be an Entrepreneur. Fourteen years later Jiang was 30 and he is working as a marketing manager for a Fortune 500 company. He didn't build any company on his own or even started to build one as he dreamt then he felt he was stuck and stagnant. He just thought about Fourteen-year-old Jiang who wrote the letter.

"It's not because I didn't try, its because every time I had a new idea, every time I want to try something new, even at work I wanted to make a proposal I wanted to speak up in front of people in a group I felt there was this constant battle between the fourteen-year-

old and six-year-old one"- Jia Jiang

At that stage Jiang started to explore within himself, he started to realize what he is and why things are like that within him, and his fear of rejection. Then he started his own company when he was thirty and he still had the fear of rejection. Later as an entrepreneur, he was put up with an investment opportunity and he was turned down. That rejection hurt him so bad that he felt like quitting right there.

He then started talking himself that any successful entrepreneur will quit for a simple investment rejection and then he felt he can build a better company, better product, and better team. Before that he can be a better leader and better person. He decided that he cannot let that six-year-old kid dictate his life anymore

This is exactly what anyone has to do to achieve something big. Understand yourself, know your fears, flaws, reactions, and character and that's when you get the opportunity to build up yourself and make yourself a better person. A person who should be capable of trusting in achieving your dream. Once you are out of your Trust illusion then work on yourself.

Jia Jiang then explored all the ways which will help him to overcome his fear of rejection. He went through many psychological articles, and rah rah inspiration articles, and after a lot of searches, he found a website named *rejectiontherapy.com* which was the game created by the Canadian entrepreneur named Jason comely. The concept of that game is to go out for thirty days and look for rejections so that every day you will be rejected at something and by the end, you desensitize yourself from the pain.

Jiang loved that idea and decided to film himself being rejected Hundred days he had his rejection ideas and wanted to make a video blog out of it.

On day one, He decided to borrow $100 from a stranger. At Jiang's workplace, he went downstairs and saw a big guy sitting at his desk Jiang was walking long and sweating and all of a sudden he asked, Hello sir, can I borrow $100 from you? And the stranger looked at him and said No! Why? Jiang was so tense and said I'm sorry and ran away from there with embarrassment as he was filming himself rejecting. At night, Jiang felt that the stranger guy was not that bad, he even asked why? Which he had a chance of explaining, and negotiating. But he just ran. Then he decided no matter what happened tomorrow I'm not going to run. I'll stay engaged.

This is what makes everyone a better person. Improving, correcting ourselves, and trying to face the fear and deal with the fear until you overcome them.

Day two, Burger refill. After his work, he had a burger at a store and after finishing his burger he went to the store person and asked him can I get a burger refill? The respective person replied, What? Burger refill? What was that? Jiang said as you refill drinks, refill my burger. The store person rejected saying no we don't refill burgers. This time Jiang took the stand. He talked and negotiated to say I love your burgers and wanted to refill. The store person said he will talk to his manager and later informed sorry man maybe later but now we don't refill burgers. That moment was a win for Jiang. He didn't feel that bad feeling as he felt on day one just because he stayed engaged and didn't run. At that pretty moment, Jiang knew he was already learning things and making a better person of himself.

Day Three, Getting an Olympic doughnut. *Jiang stated this is where his life was turned upside down.* He went to 'Krispy Kreme A doughnut store in the southeastern part of the United States, and said Can you make me doughnuts that look like Olympic symbols, basically interlinking five doughnuts together?" Then unexpectedly the doughnut maker took Jiang so seriously. And took a piece of paper and designed and asked for colors and all and in 15 minutes she brought him the doughnuts as ordered in the Olympic symbol. Jiang was so touched and happy with that. That video became viral on the internet and Jiang became famous and was invited to a lot of talk shows and received many emails with appreciation. But Jiang didn't start this process for fame but to learn something and improve himself by overcoming rejections. Even though he learned some he continued on his 100-day program and he turned that into a project.

I learned a lot of things, I discovered so many secrets. I found If I just don't run when I get rejected, I could turn a "no" into a "yes," and the Magic word is "Why."
-Jia Jiang

Jia Jiang explored and found everything about him and worked on how to overcome the fear and he worked for it and improved every single time in the process. He eventually became the person whom he can genuinely trust that he can achieve the goal which he has. Later he did some crazy stuff like knocking on strangers' doors and asking if I can plant this flower in your backyard? And as an answer he got a referral saying go to the neighbor she loves planting flowers. And then asked a

Starbucks person if he can be a Starbucks greeter for the day and they allowed him to greet the customers. He also had a dream to teach as he is from four generations of teachers. He went to a professor in Austin and asked him if he would teach his class? With great excitement, the professor agreed and after that class, Jiang was so satisfied that he could fulfill his dream.

This is how Jia Jiang made himself a capable man and made the strength out of his fear and now he takes rejection therapy classes, he is an author and CEO of wuju Learning which teaches rejection therapy.

"If I have the belief that I can do it, I can surely acquire the capacity to do it even if I may not have it at the beginning"
-Mahatma Gandhi

Self-trust will start when you get out of the illusion of what you think you are and start knowing what you are genuinely capable of and work on making yourself the person you should be to achieve your dream. *"Trusting yourself is trusting in your capabilities, skills, and interests. Believe in yourself that you could be the person you can trust"*. put in all the efforts to learn, improve and correct yourself. make yourself a better person with every try of improvement. Have the Willpower to work hard, and there is no one I know who failed in making themselves a better person. And after the short or long-term struggle, you will be the person who is capable of achieving your dream. Then 'Trusting yourself' makes complete sense which implies trusting your capabilities, willpower, talent, and skill. And that would lead you to conquer your dream.

"Trusting yourself is trusting your Capabilities, skills, and Interests"

Self-trust is a necessary condition of personal autonomy and self-respect. Self-trust involves a positive sense of the motivations and competence of the trusted person; a willingness to depend on him or her; and an acceptance of vulnerability. It does not preclude trust in others. A person may be correctly said to have too much self-trust; however, core self-trust is essential for functioning as an autonomous human being.

Trusting in self is very important and makes you brave, the trust should be on the abilities of your own. A bird sitting on the tree branch never believes the branch not to break. but the bird has the trust in its wings. This Trust in self is the power to the hands which sail, Trust keeps you to sail, and fuels energy, hope, and optimism. This Helps you throughout the storm.

Believe in your idea

"There is no better person to imagine a small idea turning into massive than the master in whose mind the idea was born."

Belief, Which is hardest to do because that had no proof to trust. Once you are capable and become the person you trust yourself then you have to believe in the idea or the dream you have. Don't need to believe the way, the path, or the journey. But always have faith and believe in the goal that will give you many ways to reach the top.

One:

If you have an idea that you truly believe is good, then you have to work on it. when the idea is born in your mind then you are the Master of that particular idea. There will be no one better than you to imagine that idea turning into a massive company, bringing a major change, creating new ways, or making an effort easier or whatever. You, the master of the idea, should believe in that idea and the rest of the world doesn't matter. To believe to this level extent, the idea of your dreams should be executed and put to work. Do not let your ideas or dreams just stay the same in your brain. Start building them boldly brick by brick, that building process is what gives you the belief that your idea is worth so much more than you think. Trust in your instincts too.

We all know one of the legends in the world *'Jeff Bezos'*. He worked on his small idea, quitting his best jobs. Bezos was the youngest *senior vice president at D.E. Shaw, a wall street hedge fund.* Just imagine a Thirty-year-old man quitting the best job that so many people worry their whole life about not being able to get that job. When a person is thirty years old, how many responsibilities will he have? I fucking wonder how much Bezos must have believed in the idea he has which gave him the courage for quitting his best job. This is not the only thing wondered me in the journey of Bezos,

Bezos selected the name of his company by referring to a dictionary after a few stops at a few names he finally settled on *'Amazon'* Because it was a place that was 'exotic and different, just as he had envisioned for his Internet enterprise. The Amazon River, he noted, was the largest in the world and he planned to make his bookstore the biggest bookstore in the world. This is how big Bezos foresaw his small idea in his mind. The Amazon is the biggest river in the world. to name a small company that is running in a garage, how much belief in the idea or in the dream anyone should have. Well, no doubt Bezos trusts himself that he will execute his idea and work hard to make his company a success. But he believed in it differently and that is how a master of the idea has to think and believe.

Two:

In this world when you have a great idea or a dream to achieve and of course, you are talented and capable enough of executing or making it a success but you cannot do it all by yourself without any leads. You will need investors to trust you, you will need directors to cast you, you will need producers to produce your music or your show, you will need clients to give you projects, and so on. *It's never so easy, and yes of course it's never impossible.* That is the major phase of the storm every person with a dream has to sail. Believing in your idea and trusting in yourself that you can make it possible when everyone around you lets you down and don't believe in your idea or you.

"I've known a lot of people that were very successful because no one else believed in them, but I don't know anyone that's ever been successful if they didn't believe in

themselves. See you can be successful if other people don't believe in you. You can overcome those odds in that opposition, but if you don't believe in yourself, no way. You just aren't gonna make it."
-Bill Clinton

It's tough when you get into a situation where someone has to believe in your idea. Because no one will. And this is the phase where a large percentage of people chase their dreams and sail the storms turn down. This is sometimes psychological discouragement when people around us or the people who need to believe in your idea and they don't, that will affect an individual's belief and turn it into doubts, What If's, maybe's. People who cannot hold their belief in their ideas or dreams are mostly not capable of executing. They feel it's a good idea but they don't trust themselves that they can make it possible and they don't take risks. So no matter how good the idea can be, you need to be capable of building it. And when you trust yourself that you can make it then no one could ever stop you from your goal with discouragements.

There are few people with ideas that no one ever trusted and now the same ideas have made them legends in today's world. People also said their ideas are lame. Jack Ma Yun, is a Chinese business magnate, investor, and philanthropist. The former executive chairman of Alibaba Group, a multinational technology conglomerate. Jack Ma Yun is mostly known as 'Jack ma.' He made himself a capable person when he was young and he trusted himself that he could execute his ideas and make them a success. The ideas Jack used to get are never accepted or believed by anyone even the people with great knowledge and wisdom in those days. Jack started his entrepreneur journey to change the world, and yes his ideas did change the world around him. He started the Alibaba company which operates through the internet. In the days when there was no scope for the internet, jack foresaw the world growing so fast and stepped into internet things and for that idea, people laughed at jack that this is never going to be successful and Alibaba after sailing through tough storms for many years Jack finally sailed Alibaba to the shore and it was damn successful. Later Jack introduced online payments for which the world around him again started laughing at him and now there are millions of payments being done every minute by the same people. People used to call him "Crazy Jack" for the ideas he has. All these insults and discouragements never made Jack quit or give up on his dream or the idea he believed in. That is the type of belief someone should hold to reach the destination.

Three:

Jack was introducing ideas that no one ever saw coming and if you think that is the reason people didn't accept or believed them then you are wrong, People don't believe the concept of ideas and it doesn't matter if the person behind the idea or the dream has got any experience or he is new to the field or he is a professional. No matter who the person is and what the idea is, the majority of people don't believe in your idea. They can sometimes trust you when you have already proved and now you are up with something new and there are chances people could trust you but never believe in your ideas. Ideas are strange, every one of us will be producing plenty of ideas every day. A three-year-old kid will have many ideas within him every day. Winning or achieving does not depend on the idea. It is completely dependent on execution. The way you execute your idea matters. This is the reason we had our first topic as trust and then belief. To believe in your idea, you need to trust that you are capable of bringing your idea into existence.

Even in those situations when people don't believe you even if you prove to them you are good at what you are doing, and no investor believes in your idea, no producer or no director or whoever it could be, even then if you believe in your idea, just do not let the words or opinions of anyone around you destroy your belief. Just keep building, keep sailing cause some people are successful when they did not stop sailing or chasing their dreams when they got rejected because their idea is not believable to succeed.

Rowan Atkinson,

There is no one who doesn't know this person 'Rowan Sebastian Atkinson globally. Rowan is mostly remembered by people as Mr.Bean who won millions of hearts by entertaining.

Atkinson was born in Consett, County Durham, England, on 6 January 1955. The youngest of four boys, Atkinson was brought up Anglican and was educated at DurhamChoristers School, a preparatory school, and then at St. Bees school. Rodney, Rowan, and their older brother Rupert were brought up in Consett and went to school with the future Prime Minister, Tony Blair, at Durham Choristers. After receiving top grades in science A levels he secured a place at Newcastle University, where he received a degree in Electrical and Electronic Engineering. In 1975, he continued for the degree of MSc in Electrical Engineering at Queen's College, Oxford, the same college where his father matriculated in 1935, and which made Atkinson an Honorary fellow in 2006.

During his college, Atkinson developed a passion for acting and he decided to be an actor.

Atkinson briefly embarked on doctoral work before devoting his full attention to acting First winning national attention in The oxford revue at the Edinburgh festival fringe in August 1976, he had already written and performed sketches for shows in Oxford by the Etceteras – the revue group of the Experimental theatre club (ETC) – and for the Oxford university dramatic club(OUDS), meeting writer Richard Curtis and compose Howard Goodall, with whom he would continue to collaborate during his career.

Atkinson starred in a series of comedy shows for BBC Radio 3 in 1979 called *The Atkinson People*. It consisted of a series of satirical interviews with fictional great men, who were played by Atkinson himself. The series was written by Atkinson and Richard Curtis and produced by Griff Rhys Jones.

In making that radio show a success Atkinson wanted to move toward his dream As he wished to become an actor.

After university, Atkinson did a one-off pilot for London weekend television in 1979 called *Canned laughter*. Atkinson then went on to do "Not the nine o'clock news" for the BBC, produced by his friend John Lloyd.

The success of *Not the Nine O'Clock News* led to him taking the lead role of Edmund Blackadder in *Blackadder*. The first series *The Black Adder* (1983), set in the medieval period, Atkinson co-wrote with Richard Curtis. After a three-year gap, in part due to budgetary concerns, a second series was broadcast, written by Curtis and Ben Elton, Blackadder 2 (1986) followed the fortunes of one of the descendants of Atkinson's original character, this time in the Elizabethan era. The same pattern was repeated in the two sequels *Blackadder the third* (1987), and *Blackadder goes forth* (1989), set in World War I. The *Blackadder* series became one of the most successful of all BBC situation comedies, spawning television specials including *Blackadder's Christmas carol* (1988), *and Blackadder the cavalier years.* (1988), and later *Blackadder back and forth* (1999), which was set at the turn of the Millennium. The final scene of "Blackadder Goes Forth"

After these many hit shows which are well successful and now Atkinson is well experienced to hold a show alone and as he was so confident and interested to do more and more series of acting then he came up with a new concept for a show. He wrote everything and Made everything ready about Mr.Bean, then started visiting the production offices and TV show offices and he was rejected by all of them. The reasons are one, the concept of Mr.Bean, and two, the stammering problem of Atkinson. After a lot of struggle and sailing, Atkinson started the Show all by himself. Just imagine He is well experienced in the same field of work, he made the previous shows a success yet, no one believed in him or the idea he has. And at that time starting all by himself, how much Atkinson should be sure about it, how much he must have trusted himself and believed in his idea.

Atkinson did make Mr.bean all by himself and, Mr.Bean was a global hit. Every kid from every corner of the world loved the show and it was a massive success. Just not kids, everyone who watched the show used to enjoy it.

It's not just Atkinson, there are many legends whose ideas were once rejected because no one believed in their idea. Walt Disney, J.K. Rowling, Jack Ma, and plenty more personalities did not let the opinion of the other destroy their confidence and they always believed in their idea and trusted themselves to make it through. When you truly believe in something, it's crazy. Don't expect the world to believe you or your idea, the world never offers you the belief in whatever you are doing. In the big run the only belief you will have is yours, and always trust your abilities, if they are not up to the mark trust them then just work on them, improve them and then hold the trust.

"Trust and belief are the fuels for a sailing boat. The more you have them, the farther and stronger you can sail".

DON'T SNOOZE YOUR DREAMS

"Snoozing alarm is losing dream"

Alarm, which plays a crucial role in everyone's life today. I have read an article on the internet, it's the study on the relationship between alarm and the snooze button.

There is 27.12 percent of people anxious when their alarm goes off, While only 11.24 percent feel energized, 2.32 percent feel excited and 0.32 percent feel awake the remaining feels either annoyed, tired, resigned, or angry. So If hearing your alarm in the morning doesn't exactly have you happily jumping out of bed, you're in the majority. Annoyed and angry? Was it not the alarm they set for their schedule? In this study, I felt people who feel energized and excited have the real purpose of waking up. It doesn't matter if they slept for 5 hours or just half an hour but they still have a real purpose in their life and they feel responsible for that and they feel excited to wake up.

And about the snooze button, the Majority of people hit snooze at least once. A little more than one-third 35.57 percent of women and 43.39 percent of men say they never hit snooze, with the rest admitting to hitting snooze at least once. As for chronic snoozers, 6.31 percent of women and 5.65 percent of men say they snooze more than three times. Dividing by generation, millennials(Who are born in the early 1980s and 1990s) are the least likely to hit snooze, 57.31 percent never do.

Two kinds of people who hit snooze, One are mostly lazy, that they have work and they knew they have to wake up but they still want a little more sleep and Two, People who are on a long term working hours and took little rest they will hit snooze because that 5 or 10 minutes sleep is a real charge for those people who are working hard.

In the early days of my entrepreneurial journey, I used to set up an alarm at whatever time I scheduled according to the work and tasks I had the next day. And Of course, I was among the majority of people. In fact, I set the alarm four times every ten minutes and snooze every single time I hear the alarm ringing. And definitely, I used to get up at least 30 or 40 minutes late according to my scheduled timetable. And one fine day in my area where I'm trying to scale up my business with advertising, as usual, I woke up 40 mins late for which I was habituated to standing on my balcony and saw a large group of people walking back to their homes. Those people are large in number and they are between 28 to 50 years old who are the people we targeted to advertise (Our target of the market). And I felt like my opportunities of the day was walking back home and I lost them.

The very next day my only target for the day is to get up exactly at 6 and without any snoozing, I've failed to do that. This means I lost the opportunities of that day too, and I have decided to play the game differently. For the next day, I set my alarm 3 times every 20 minutes, but this time I've set it from 5 AM to 6 AM for which my schedule is to wake up at 6 AM. Yes, somehow I managed to wake up and went into the market to see what was happening and how I can advertise to the people who are rushing in their work.

That day, I have seen plenty of opportunities not just for advertising but there are many I can cash in but all I was doing is snoozing all of them all these days. Then for a few more days, I used the same trick to wake up early and in just a week I was very busy in my morning schedule and I didn't need the alarm to wake me up anymore. My responsibilities, My tasks, and work, and My dreams wake me up. Then I realized, All the days I was snoozing my alarm is not just as simple as a snoozing alarm for just 10 minutes, it was snoozing my dreams for the next day and the opportunities for a few more weeks or some of them are like I can never get them again. Then I saw great things happening with just 5 mins early wake-up and then I started getting up at 5 AM.

This is not just about waking up early, I took it as an example because that is one of the important lessons I've learned that a snoozing alarm for 10 mins is snoozing your dream for so far which takes longer to reach. For all the people who have really big dreams or the goals to achieve and you are at the point that you have to start executing but you are snoozing them for next year or next month or next day, Remember,

**"Feedbacks and reviews belong to yesterday,
Winning and losing belong to tomorrow,
Decisions and execution belong to today".
And that today is always 'Now'.**

Yesterday was forever yesterday, Tomorrow will always be tomorrow, all you have is Today, Which is now this exact point in time. There is never *"Get set Go tomorrow" there is always "Get Set Go"*. Oh well, It's so damn easy to just write a couple of lines saying don't postpone your dreams, Do it now, make a decision. But it's a very tough step to do. It's just a turn in the walk of your life that will for sure change the destination. So it's not simple, you ought to be scared to make that decision. But all you have to think about is not whether it was a simple decision or a tough decision. Just know if that decision is worth what it brings you, whether you are ready to work hard in that way you choose, whether you are ready to take the rejections, learn every day, lose many times and wake up fresh every next morning and grind every single day until you make it.

**There is never "Get set Go tomorrow" there
is always "Get Set Go"**

Hindrance

Why and what stops anyone to take that one step towards their dream. It's their dream, Goal, that's what they love and want to achieve, and yet, why does anyone keep postponing it.

There are just three main hindrances that cover plenty of them.

Fear of being strange

When you want to start something which lightens up your future when you know you can make it happen then why do you care how it looks to the world? Why do you fear thinking it is strange? It's not strange, It's unique. This is your life, Your dream, and your career, and do it for yourself without any hesitation about what people will be stating and how the world will react to it. Being unique for a while is fine until everything which seems unique turns into something that brings great results and happiness for you. According to psychology, Uniqueness seeking allows people to attain satisfaction with their specialness. Also, uniqueness seeking may increase the diversity in society. This happens because the people with high needs for uniqueness seek different goals and interests, and in doing so, they open up new arenas in which other people can succeed. observe that having a personal sense of uniqueness allows people more freedom to make lifestyle choices, as opposed to relying on others for points of reference. They recognize that feeling unique means feeling special while walking down one's path, rather than seeking to conform to external influences.

**"Be different so that people can see you
clearly amongst the crowds"
-Mehmet Murat ildan**

Fear of capability

According to me, People who have Fear of capabilities have more chances of winning or making it. This category of people has more possibilities than people who think I can do but lack capabilities. If you fear your capabilities then that's not a disadvantage but that's an advantage that has an opportunity to turn into winning. It is very hard to know your capabilities but when you already doubt them or have fear of them, now all you have to do is to work on them, improve your capabilities, and make yourself more capable. What will be the best thing in starting a business or startup or whatsoever that you know your dream and what to do and what capabilities you have and you also doubt them? So it's as simple as it is to work on them and make yourself capable enough to achieve your dream. Capabilities are doubted when there is no clarity on what barriers are going to hit on the way. And no one ever could say what are the barriers coming on the way. So being more capable by improving your abilities is all it takes. People who have the fear of their capabilities, can improve themselves and will execute the work with more cautiousness. Without any over confidence.

> *"All human beings have the capability of*
> *doing what they want,*
> *what they're attracted to"*
> *-Jack Kirby*

Fear of failure

The world runs only in one way, when you still have the chance in your hand, take it or lose it. There is no other way to postpone the chance or the opportunities you have. Well winning and losing is just not what you have to concentrate on when you start, All you have to do is sail, keep going, keep changing the flopping plans and executing the new ones, and get going. Make yourself smarter, learn every small thing in every little failure, and get stronger. then you will not fear failure as you are more capable of winning.

Excluding people who are not sure if they will ever start executing their dreams if it's just an idea in their heads. If you are so damn sure you will want to start your business or startup or skill-based profession or traveling or whatsoever and if you are postponing the 'start' to tomorrow just with the fear of failure then you are just postponing your fear and failure not the start.

There is something I have learned in early failures of my sailing, As every one of us knows there is either *'Winning or Losing'* But we can change that. Yes, I said it correctly. I found that we can change that. In Fact, there are legends out there who tried changing that and they made it. It's 'Winning or Trying again'. Just don't cut off your energy thinking what? Trying again? Another shot of struggle? No, This is the formula that made failing people into successful legends in world history. Well, I came to the conclusion that I can skip failing or losing by 'Trying again'.

"Fear kills more dreams than failure ever will"
-Suzy Kassen

Right of the second dream

Dreams, It feels so good dreaming about something great, something rich, and something that you love. But we are talking about the dreams to pursue not dreams wishing to happen but the dreams you are ready to work hard for to achieve or to conquer something big. We have dreams that mean real dreams, sometimes we have more than one dream that could be not just two or three but just as many as you dream of. But the very first is always the hardest. That is where you learn the stuff, you know yourself more, you build yourself differently and that will be like the armor for yourself in all aspects.

Achieving the first dream will be the toughest sail ever. Well pursuing a job is not a dream but working hard as an employee to reach some targeted cadre in that office by 'X' years is a dream. Being a student is not a dream but studying the course on purpose, researching or taking projects, and learning to the depths of the topics to achieve something is a dream. Learning music is not a dream, learning music because you are looking forward to becoming a music director or a musician or whatever and the process of this learning is called chasing the dream. There is always a difference between Interests, Hobbies, Responsibilities, Works, Jobs, and Dreams.

As we are looking into those real dreams, If you have more than one dream and you are thinking or planning to execute them simultaneously then know the Rights of your second dream.

You can dream enough dreams but do not get to execute a second dream until you sail your first one to shore. Few people try implementing their other dreams simultaneously when their first one is not doing well. Things happen badly but change the plan, fail, change the plan again, and do it again until you get the way to shore but do not be in an illusion that implementing another big dream could help you or lead you to success. Because it does take a lot of determination to start executing your dream, a lot of groundwork, and concentration. Dedicating time to different dreams will make all of them suffer a bit, you always need to be fully invested and focused on each goal. If you split all your investment, energy, and focus on each damn thing then it might lead both the valuable dreams to drown.

Here we can take the concept of Will Smith's notion That a plan B will only distract you from plan A. But here we are looking into dreams as in projects. But the context from that notion can be applied here for dreams and goals. That will be thrillingly similar for understanding by just replacing 'Plan' with 'Dreams'. So, The right of a second dream is to let the dream one reach the shore.

SMARTNESS IS CROWN

"Think smart, act smart, Get smart, Grow smarter"

Smart, This is the crown in whatever field you want to excel. Well, to clear the little confusion there is a difference between intelligence and smartness, Intelligence is what we are born with. The ability to think and how fast we can process the brian. Smartness is what we improve day to day in a particular subject by learning new ways and new things deep in what we are inspired by. Also could be in questioning and answering.

There has been a myth for ages that all of us have believed that being smart is something that is fixed and measured by things like IQ, SATs, GPA, or highest degree according to a few people. We have been misunderstanding that we are born with some 'X' IQ and that is fixed and will not change. Sandra Bond Chapman is a **cognitive neuroscientist**, founder, and chief director of the Centre for BrainHealth, Dee Wyly Distinguished

Professor in Brain Health, and a professor in the School of Behavioural and Brain Sciences at The University of Texas at Dallas. Sandra Chapman on a Ted talk in 2013 stated *"We can make our brains smarter"* which was proved and it's a science faction but not science fiction anymore. IQ was never designed to measure the highest bar our brain could achieve. Smart is more than IQ.

When we use the frontal lobe of the brain, we can make our brain healthier. Using the frontal lobe or a part of the brain is not something strange. It's just you have to think in higher-level ways to engage your brain. Sandra Chapman very clearly explained the strategies which she called brain powers in her ted talk.

The Brainpower of one:

This is where you single-mindedly focus on one thing and avoid the tasks of doing two things at once and you don't let distractions come in.

The Brainpower of two:

This is where you look at the long list of all the work you have to do and you figure out what are the two most important things that are going to make the most difference in your day and you spend your brain's prime time doing those.

The Brainpower of deep:

This requires the most effort, this is where you take the information from all the sources and blend it with the rich knowledge that's already there and form abstracted ideas, and general ideas, and then synthesize them constantly throughout the day.

The Brainpower of less:

Reduce the amount of information. Big data freeze our brains. Our brain's connections happen faster when we do the things we are inspired by. Then eating, and sleeping is two main things that keep our brain healthy.

So now it's very clear that no one of us is dumb. It all depends on how well you use your intelligence and get smarter in whatever work you do or whatever dream you want to achieve. Well, science also proved that our brain connections happen pretty much faster when we work on something we are inspired by, something we are interested in. It all depends on interest, focus, the hunger for success, and the desire to think in different areas and find many other ways. Become a Smart ass, and that will be so much helpful in your sail. Smart work can always take over hard work. If you are not smart that's not an issue because you can still make yourself smarter.

Work harder to find smarter ways

No matter how hard you work, there will always be a greater reward for the one who works smart. Because smart work always beats hard work. Working hard is putting arduous days and nights into doing one or multiple tasks. Working smart is finding effective and efficient ways to complete one or multiple tasks while managing time and quality at the same time. Hard Work alone does so little, smart work alone doesn't take u to accomplish the task or tasks. When you find the smarter ways, smarter solutions, and smarter processes and work hard for them, that is when you make your sail easier than other ways. You will be capable of sailing the toughest storm on the day you can combine hard work and smart work.

One day two young woodcutters Mike and Steve have started their wood cutting business sharing a workplace. Clients for both Mike and Steve have been coming and both of them are getting good enough projects. After a few weeks, there is a talk spread around that village that Mike is delivering on time for his customers and he is never late or he never asks for one more day to finish the wood cuttings.

Slowly a few clients from Steve are giving their next orders to mike. And Mike never disappoints his client and he is always on time. Steve figures out his customers are going to Mike and Mike's business is vastly improving and Steve is losing his customers. He gave a lot of thought and he decided to observe how come Mike can do the work so quickly when Steve himself works so hard all day and on a few days he works himself more than mike does but still he cannot keep up on time. The next day Steve started his work at the same time as Mike and Steve started observing Mike while working he found that Mike is stopping his work every one hour. Take a break for ten minutes. Mike did this all the week and Steve worked continuously without any breaks also he worked two hours more than Mike did. Yet, After a week Steve saw that Mike did better work than him. Steve was frustrated because after putting in all the hard work more than Mike, how could he not be rewarded more than mike.

Out of curiosity Steve walked to Mike and asked, How can you do this? You are taking a break for every one hour and working two hours less than me and still, your output is more? Mike replied, Yes, you are working harder than me. But how long has it been since you sharpened your axe? Steve replied, one year. Mike said Every time I take a break I sharpen my axe a bit until it's perfect to cut. And that's how I can cut faster.

This is what matters. When you are at work you should be smart in what you are doing. To be smart, You should know exactly what you are doing and gain complete knowledge of the work or the process. Then think of all the major areas you should concentrate on, think differently and find smarter ways, then work hard in those ways. The rewards are going to be amazing.

Working hard? How hard is it?

One of my friend's dad drives Auto Rickshaw for a living, and I also know a guy who lives at the end of my street and his dad drives an auto-rickshaw for a living too. Both of them have been running their families by driving auto-rickshaws for around Twenty or twenty-five years. They still do the same but the difference is both the families are financially quite opposite, the lifestyle of those two families is in contrast to each other.

My college mate is always so cool, relaxed, and never stressed about his family's financial conditions. He has a good phone and bike and he never spends money on worthless things but when we hang out together he always takes money from his pocket to pay. He could buy anything which he wants and of course, if it's useful for studies or career or whatever good and productive. And he never used to tell me my dad stays all day outside working hard. Whenever I talk to his father I feel he is a smart person. On the other hand, the guy at the end of my street always talks about his family's financial condition saying it's worse, I have no money, no matter how hard my dad is working by staying all day out and yet he cannot make more money. He used to tell this to many people on the street who are his friends, and also to people who know him.

So I was so confused. How is this happening? Both of them live in the same city and do the same work. This means both of them should have the same opportunity and then the result should also be the same. But why is it in contrast? So I asked my college mate what is your father's schedule for the day? He replied, He wakes up at 5 AM, and gets milk from the dairy which we will sell to people in our street. It's just a one-hour thing. Then he takes a bath and will start to pick up school kids at 6 AM and drop all of them at school at 8.30 AM he takes two trips. From 8.30 AM he will be on the college and office routes where there are so many people who need an auto rickshaw and reach home by 11 AM. He spends all afternoon at home reading the newspaper and doing some work at home. Again in the evening, he will go pick up school kids and drop them at their places and he will be on college and Office routes till 8 PM and gets back home by 8.30 PM. He earns 1500 Rs per day on average. Then on the other hand when I saw the person on the street I asked him what is his father's schedule, He said he will wake up at 7 in the morning, He will bath, have breakfast, and step out of home at around 9.30 AM, He will park his auto-rickshaw in a stand-in our area and waits for the customers to come till afternoon. He goes home for a lunch break at 1 PM and rests till evening and gets back to the same parking stand at 5 PM. He will be there waiting for customers till 9 PM. Some days he will not take a rest in the afternoon, and as soon as he finishes lunch he will go back to the parking stand. He may earn 250 Rs per day. He said this process and ended by saying he works hard staying all day out but even then he is not able to make enough money.

I was amazed by these both processes, Hard Work is not actually hard work. But working a bit smarter and grabbing the opportunity of the market shows a really big change in the rewards. Both of them think they work hard, but my college mate's father is happy with the rewards he is gaining for his hard work and he is satisfied and that struggle doesn't make him feel he is working so hard so he never mentions my dad working so hard and all. But the father of the guy in my street considers themself working hard and yet does not make any rewards. So even after all day spends by waiting for customers it still makes him feel like he is working hard.

How important Is smartness in whatever work you do? Being smart is really rewarding and don't consider yourself working hard if there are not enough rewards coming. Just analyze the process in full knowledge of what you are doing, look up to all the opportunities you have, then make a smarter way, and that is when you have to work hard. Just because you put in plenty of hours in work you don't get the rewards, Be a little smarter and then grow.

"Be smart enough to analyze the risks worth taking"

Risks, The word which frightens us. Well, What precious things in this world will reach you without any risk? You should risk your 9 to 5 job to start a business or startup, You should risk your dream to feed your family, you should risk your family to quit your job to do what makes you happy, and you should risk important relations in your life to go far for studies or to work, we can keep on saying cause world lets every life runs with risks. So, nothing in life we can earn without risking something or the other.

But for the people who are chasing their dreams, sailing the storms, they have to make tough calls often. Every decision is pretty serious in their journey and 80% of decisions route to risks. When you are on the hunt for your goal then you should know what risks to take. You should be smart enough to analyze the risks worth taking. Analyzing if that particular risk is worth taking or doesn't worth taking you to need to be experienced, to be experienced you need to be failed. But if you are in the early stages of building your dream(Like me), then analyzing the risks is a real tough part which I have experienced when I was in that situation to take a call. But here is something which can help a lot, Foresee the results in multiple ways and multiple scenarios.

Chess could be the best example of analyzing the risks. In chess, players have to make moves and every move completely depends on the full game. So the players, no matter how new player you are, if you are familiar with the rules then the second thing which anyone does automatically without anyone teaching in chess is guessing the counter moves from the opponent. Before moving from one end, the player will go through the opponent's counter moves in many ways and predict what could be the counter move. Well, chasing your dream is not like playing chess for a while. But when you see carefully, whenever you play chess it's always about winning. You don't play for entertainment or fun, you always play to win. So during the time of the game you'll think, predict, and analyze, So, it's just like playing a serious chess match. Foresee the ways where your decision leads, how many possibilities, how many barriers, how many disadvantages, how many maybe's, may not's, if's, and so many like this.

Remember when you lose the chess game you end up with nothing lost but If it's in your sail or the chase be more cautious, more attentive, and prepare solutions for all the ifs, maybes, and may not beforehand.

Being smart is nothing but thinking from all directions and making the best spontaneous decisions and split responses which were explained above. Every entrepreneur, businessman, and skill-based professional says risks are part of their journey, But to analyze them has no tricks and no shortcuts. You should learn by yourself. Know what exactly you're doing, believe in your idea, trust the process, and be ready to face the counters from that risk. And you will make the good calls or in worst cases, you will be ready to face the counters with the moves you already planned and prepared.

Ratan Tata has decided to step into the automobile industry to manufacture and produce its cars which is a very risky task. When he shared his decision with his friends overseas who are in the automobile business said this could not be done. We have to go through a collaboration to get technology and all whichever is needed. it's impossible to execute this project individually which involves unbearable risks. But Ratan Tata did not turn back after he decided to launch TATA motors, he said when I was involved in this automobile industry and in the works of launching Indica cars I felt there is no friend for me. He said this because no one supported him in this process. After all, it involves risk. After the launch of the Indica car from TATA motors which is full of Indian content, it was a hit in the market. Acquired 20% market share. This proves Ratan tata analyzed Risk which is worth taking. And worked hell hard to make it happen. Yes, it needs a lot to be able to analyze risks worth taking and make yourself a capable person to handle those tough phases.

"If you are not willing to risk the unusual, you will have to settle for the ordinary"
-Jim Rohn

Get smarter

How smart are you? To answer this question we think we need a group of people to compare. That is when we can be able to figure out we are smarter than them and not smarter than them. You can never tell how smart someone is, But you do know how smart you are. How smart you are today, How smart you were yesterday. So, to be smarter every day just explore within yourself every single day with every small situation and daily circumstance.

"Be smarter than yesterday, you should be able to tell it every day."

Exercise your brain, keep thinking better than yesterday, create more ways in your work, make easier solutions for your problems, solve puzzling situations and yes you will be smarter every day. Only you know yourself better than anyone else in this world. So be honest to yourself in the first place and make yourself smarter than every passing moment and repeat it every single day. You can be smarter every day. There are few productive habits and a quality way of living that helps you to get smarter day by day.

The way we think, the habits we adopt, and the productivity we maintain all together make a quality of life. Based on all of those the way we react to situations and the decisions in daily life and long-term decisions makes us a smart person. Improving the process to the best makes us smarter.

Smartness is all about handling your thoughts, staying present, calm and focused even in the critical situations. Thinking out of box and decoding the various solutions for a single problem and making the best way out of it. In the world business smartest people in the department of marketing and public relations manuplate the psycology of the public. Handling or attracting others mind, thoughts and creating them opinions on things around is is different type of smartness. Well, we cannot finish the chapter about topic "Smart" without learning something about the smartest person whose tactics and techniques in marketing and public relation are being followed till date,The father of PR (Public relation)

Edward Louis Bernays

Edward Louis Bernays was an American theorist, considered a pioneer in the field of public relations and propaganda, and referred to in his obituary as "the father of public relations". Bernays was named one of the 100 most influential Americans of the 20th century by Life

"We are governed, Our minds are molded, our tastes are formed, our ideas are suggested."
-Edward Bernays

The Biography of an Idea: Memoirs of Public Relations Counsel is the book written by Edward, in which all his world, ideas, and stories are mentioned. You may also want to read Bernay's Propaganda and Crystallizing Public Opinion.

In the 1920s, America's luggage industry was worried that Americans were buying less and smaller luggage. They asked Bernays for help In response, Bernays:

Sent articles to magazines titled What the Well Dressed Woman Wears on a Weekend. These stressed the need for women to travel with a varied wardrobe and advised hostesses to stress in their invitations the different sorts of activities their guests would be involved with – and the need for different clothes for each activity.

He gave the luggage to movies and plays. suggested health officials emphasize the importance that a person should own their own luggage. He asked textile or clothing stores to put luggage in window displays(which is being successfully working to date), to show the relationship between new clothes styles and new luggage styles. He wrote to colleges and universities to send their new intake lists of the clothes and luggage they would need before arriving. He created the Luggage Information Service, to be an easy point of call for any journalist or salesperson who wanted to know more about luggage. (The growth of customer information service). Urged architects to allot suitable space for luggage storage. wrote to 66 railway companies, and 10 steamship companies and urged them to make sure their designers left plenty of room for luggage keeping in mind the importance and growth of luggage. And he lobbied foreign embassies to help increase the free weight allowance for those traveling abroad. Gave movie luggage, and had them pose with it. All these smart moves helped the sale of the luggage industry. Bernays never directly concentrates on telling the customer to buy stuff instead, he manipulates the public and attracts them in different ways.

One of the smartest works of Edward in world history which changed the entire view of the public and brought great changes around the globe is in the tobacco industry.

Before the twentieth-century smoking was seen as a habit that was corrupt and inappropriate for women. Dutch painters used cigarettes as a symbol of human foolishness in the 17th century and the 19th century, cigarettes were perceived as props for "Fallen women" and prostitutes. Women's smoking was seen as immoral and some states tried to prevent women from smoking by enforcing laws. In 1904 a woman named Jennie Lasher was sentenced to thirty days in jail for putting her children's morals at risk by smoking in their presence and in 1908 the Newyork city Board of Aldermen unanimously passed an ordinance that prohibited smoking by women in public. Similarly, in 1921 a bill was proposed to prohibit women from smoking in the district of Columbia Some women's groups also fought against women smoking. The International tobacco league lobbied for filmmakers to refrain from putting women smoking cigarettes in movies unless the women being portrayed were of "discreditable" character and other women's groups asked young girls to sign pledges saying that they would not use tobacco. These groups saw smoking as an immoral activity and a threat.

Cigarette companies began selectively advertising to women in the late 1920s In 1928 George Washington hill, the president of the American tobacco company, realized the potential market that could be found in women and said, "It will be like opening a gold mine right in our front yard." Yet some women who were already smoking were seen as smoking incorrectly.on those tough days for women to smoke, To expand the number of women smokers Hill decided to hire Edward Bernays, to help him recruit women smokers. Bernays decided to attempt to eliminate the social taboo against women smoking in public. He gained advice from psychoanalyst A.A.Brill, who stated that it was normal for women to smoke because of oral fixation and said, "Today the emancipation of women has suppressed many of their feminine desires. More women now do the same work as men do. Many women bear no children; those who do bear have fewer children. Feminine traits are masked. Cigarettes, which are equated with men, become torches of freedom. In 1929 Bernays made cigarettes re the torches of freedom for women and decided to pay women to smoke their "torches of freedom" as they walked in the Easter Sunday parade in New York. This was a shock because, until that time, women were only permitted to smoke in certain places such as in the privacy of their own homes. He was very careful when picking women to march because "while they should be good looking, they should not look too model-y" and he hired his own photographers to make sure that good pictures were taken and then published around the world. Feminist Ruth hale also called for women to join in the march saying, "Women! Light another torch of freedom! Fight another sex taboo!" Once the footage was released, the campaign was being talked about everywhere, and the women's walk was seen as a protest for equality and sparked discussion throughout the nation and is still known today. The targeting of women in tobacco advertising by bernay is pretty manipulative, he made the advertising psychologically and manipulated with help of feminism which led to higher rates of smoking among women. In 1923 women only purchased 5% of cigarettes sold; in 1929 that percentage increased to 12%, in 1935 to 18.1%, peaking in 1965 at 33.3%, and remaining at this level until 1977.

Later in 1934, George Washington hill asked Bernays for help again, he wants more, more, and more women to smoke his company's Lucky strikes and Bernays made it happen again with his intellectual tactics.

There are many smart moves by the father of PR in his journey and he will forever be a great inspiration in public relations.

Know the difference between working hard and making a normal work feels hard, find all your efforts and hard work to find smarter ways in whatever you are doing and stay focused on those smart ways, be cautious at every move and never forget that you can get smarter with every next move and next plan.

Source, The above paragraphs were referred from wikipedia:Torches of freedom

DESTINATION IS IMPORTANT

"If a man knows not which port he sails,
no wind is favorable"
- Seneca

The destination is what you have set to reach as your goal. Of Course, the destination doesn't mean to be the last stop of the journey, it could be a milestone too, it is something that brought you a long way without diversions. The destination is important because it helps you to look at something from far and find ways and directions to reach that particular point. A lighthouse could be an example. The destination is not only the stage that you should reach, it could also be a purpose to fulfill. Yes, journeys are always tough, but without a destination the journey may wither away.

"When you know the destination, you'll drive differently".

To reach your dream, you should always have a set of goals and the destination is one among them. It is a level of achievement, and there is no limit to the levels. It can make you more productive, no matter who you are until you have a dream and set of goals but once you are in the sea, you should make yourself ready to face the storm, you should make yourself more productive in the destination, stronger to sail, wiser to plan, more capable to execute. A journey makes you all these, but the purpose of the journey is always Destination.

In the journey, Every morning you wake up with a set of tasks for the day which keeps you a little forward to the goal. The entire journey takes place during the day but to keep you motivated for all the journey, For all the struggle, for all the vision, a little or too far seems your destination. Yes, you wake up with the day plans and rush into your day, but when you go to bed after a long hard day, you will always think of your destination. It feels amazing when you know where you are sailing and your destination helps you as a guide and you can see day-to-day progress. The feeling you are getting closer keeps you motivated and prepares you for the next day stronger and wiser.

"Destination helps you to track the pace of journey"

In whatever walk of life, we always keep chasing. We study to get educated, we cook to eat meals, we exercise to be fit, we work all day hard to put bread on the table, we choose different ways of career to build something, invent something, make things easy, everything whatever we do has a purpose and having purpose is important because purposes are the destination points. So for the ones who are trying to build something big in life, they should have a destination for sure. When we have a destination before us we can know how far we have reached the point and how far is left. Because in the journey or the sail, a few days we scale up the progress and a few days scale down the progress. The pace of the journey is important to always check and speed up accordingly. To know the pace of the journey you should have the destination.

The destination is the level of achievement, Ambition, Purpose, Major milestones, Dream, Aim, Change, Transmission, etc are what we work pretty hard to conquer. An athlete should know for what he is training, For what race, what sport, how many meters, and to get what, A doctor should know what is the main thing he is treating for, and A businessman should know what he wants to achieve, a student should know what degree he wants, A officer should know what is he solving for, A cook should know what he should prepare, a pilot should know where to land, sailor where to sail and everything's meant to be on track only if they know the destination, The direction depends on destination.

Once you know what you want, which is your dream and that's your destination, then begin the journey. The purpose is a destination that helps journey as the longest and brightest lighthouse ever. And for the journey to be correct on track there should be a Plan

The plan is a torch

The plan is everything we do. In a chase or a hunt for the big dreams of your life, Vision is the destination, and you will never have paths before you. All you have is a destination. Now you must make your way through the milestones all along to your dream. In this amazing journey, Plan is your torch. You cannot think to just start over and sail this without any route map, or compass which is a plan, this says you don't know what exactly you are doing. Having complete knowledge of the sail helps you to make plans for operating your mission, and makes you capable to plan for the upcoming storms in the sail. The plan is everything, Plan is never just one big thing that directly puts you at the endpoint, plans will be involved in every inch of progress. The desire to dream and the hunger to speed up the pace will let you make better and smarter plans. Never neglect to plan whatever small task it can be, only a dead fish will go in the flow.

"Only a dead fish goes with a flow"

In the chase of your dream, all you have to do is get every little work done daily which puts you a little forward to your destination. There will be a set of tasks to be done every day, every week, or at any time intervals, all you have to do is set multiple plans for all the tasks to be worked on and frame them perfectly, and then execute them accordingly. There is going to be no achievement without planning on small or big tasks. Every task which is small, big, or huge has to be planned and executed to take you closer to the destination.

"Plan helps you not to miss the path"

There is a newly married couple on their honeymoon trip, and the location is near some kind of thick bamboo forest. All the trip is going well as they planned, they are so happy spending their newly married days. On their 4-day trip, they planned to do a lot of crazy things which they can cherish for the rest of their lives. First three days they were successful in doing whatever they planned perfectly to do. On the fourth day, which is the last day of the trip, they were tired so they just planned to rest in the backyard of the resort. They were hanging out in the backyard relaxing and then the husband showed his wife the thick bamboo forest from the yard which is at a walkable distance and seemed scenic as the sun rays over it. Then the wife suggested let's go into the forest for a little walk, which we can count as one of our crazy things. Husband is not sure about it cause they prepared to rest and the forest seems pretty thick and they didn't plan anything to get in. But the wife somehow convinced her husband and they just thought they would walk in for 5 mins and return after that. Well, they started without any plan, they just kept walking for 2 mins. And they see no light and when they look back everything is dark because of the thick bamboo rush. So they decided to get back and turned around and started walking. They continuously walked for 15 mins and could not find an exit or the way they came in. And they thought to change direction a bit and walked for 30 mins yet they did not find a way out. Everything seemed similar around and then the couple began to panic. With the confusion and fear wife began to run in all directions in the thick forest. They struggled for hours to find a way out and had no use. After a few hours of struggle, the husband found they could not walk in a straight line because of thick bamboo and then he realized no matter how long they try walking everything is useless, then-husband came up with a plan, he picked up a dry bamboo from the ground which is straight and long. He pointed it opposite to the early sun raining rays, with the help of that stick they walk for one and half hours moving the stick forward and following it as it is in a perfectly straight way. In just one and half hours, they got out of the forest, unfortunately not exactly to the backyard of the resort. But still, they made their way when they had a plan and executed it.

The plan is the torch or the stick which helps you to get out of the puzzled path. If you made a plan before getting into a problem, that plan tells you the path, the odds of the small journey, the struggles of the journey, and what all hindrances may come. Plan for all of them, and make a plan ready in and for all kinds of situations. To win a situation, a plan doesn't need to be only one, there can be a mixture of plans which is the main path, for hindrances, and diverting odds all these will be under one name PLAN- Guide of the journey.

Plan to be executed, Plan to be followed

Many plans fail because all the team will be under confusion about who is following the plan and who is executing the plan. There is a difference between executing and following, when you know the exact difference and then if you work on it, Rewards are amazing.

An employee who doesn't have the authority to instruct any other employee is one of the team members who should follow the team's plan. Not the plan which he set individually for his task, but the plans that his team has set for him. Every Team leader should follow the plan which is set by the manager and to follow that plan he should make a few plans for his team and execute them. In this way, panning works. The following plan is doing the responsible duty allotted with no out focus. When you lead the team you are the one who should be fully aware of the plan and the one who is executing it. or if you are part of the team make it clear about your role in the plan, executing, or following.

No matter how good the plan is, If the team has no clarity over who is in charge of the plan, who is the one executing the plan, and who are members following the plan then the plan is going nowhere.

"It isn't a Plan until it is Planned perfectly"

One Night 4 college students were playing till late at night and could not study for the test which was scheduled for the next day. In the morning four of them thought of a plan. They made themselves look dirty with grease and dirt. They then went up to the Dean and said that they had gone out to a wedding last night and on their return, the tire of their car burst and they had to push the car all the way back and that they were in no condition to appear for the test. So the Dean said they could have the re-test after 3 days. They thanked him and said they would be ready by that time. On the third day they appeared before the Dean, the Dean said that as this was a Special Condition Test, all four were required to sit in separate classrooms for the test. They all agreed as they had prepared well in the last 3 days.

The Test consisted of 2 questions with a total of 100 Marks.

Q1. Name of the car? (2 MARKS)

Q2. Which tire burst? (98 MARKS)

The above story might be funny but in reality, the plans could backfire badly if they are not perfectly planned and executed. Plans should be planned smartly and executed very cautiously, journey is everything about plans and executions, To the very big dream needs very smart plans and brilliant execution and yet, there are chances of failing. Plans take you forward and a lot forward but may not succeed and that doesn't mean it's the end. If the plan fails, Change the plan

Change the plan

You went up with a perfect plan which has all the preplanned counters and attacks and defensive moves. You and your team have brilliantly executed and followed every responsibility. Yet the plan could fail. Yes, there are more possibilities of failing over succeeding. This doesn't mean the plan wasn't good or executing was bad and all. Well, of course, mistakes could have been made but the failure of that plan is not the end. Change the plan. Not just when the plan in progress fails, but even when the plan in progress seems to skip away, or miss the track, at those critical times make tough calls for changing the plans. In the sail when you planned to sail in one of the best boats and in half way you found the boat has damage and could sink in a couple of hours and at that moment it's just insane sticking to that plan of sailing in the same boat, change the plan, build something from scrap don't waste even a little time by expecting or wishing for the failed plan to work. A Plan has no terms & conditions like don't change or blindly follow the same plan. Executing a plan is real smart work that should be done with high cautiousness and extra care.

"Change as many plans as it needs to take you to your Dream"

The sail to your dream is the real struggle that has no compass, no directions, no intimations, and nothing. It takes a lot of courage to face the storms. There will be plans, executions, rejections, and failures again the same repeats, the same lap goes on but every new plan will be smarter, every execution will be more brilliant, every rejection makes you stronger, and every failure takes you closer to the destination. All you have to be ready for is keep planning your next move.

Plans have to be changed, plans have to be corrected, plans have to be created, and plans have to be recreated. A lot of times, Until the last plan drops you at your destination. Many successful people have experienced this in their businesses and lives. There are large companies that have just kept changing plans and strategies without accepting defeats and they have reached the point of massive success.

NESTLE

Nestle, one of the booming companies, had brought coffee to Japan post World War II with the perception of a huge market to exploit. Nestle developed an amazing product of coffee and priced it affordable, trail ran the taste well with its intended customers. But Nestle failed in selling the product. The plan was to build the best product and launch it in Japan. And everything went well but no sale was marked. The plan failed.

The company team came up with other plans in reacting to the conditions, the Advertising plan didn't work, and failed. And the next plan is Sampling, which did not work either, and failed. And they planned promotions which also failed. Nestle kept on facing the struggle and changing plans to make the sales, everything they planned and executed is not working.

Japan was a tea-drinking nation. People over there don't know about coffee. No one knows how coffee tastes. The brand managers of Nestle were puzzled and frustrated.

Nestle tried all the plans, but they got nothing working and they didn't give up. They wanted someone who can suggest a smarter plan so, In 1975, the famous French psychoanalyst, **Clotaire Rapaille,** was invited to Japan by Nestle. Rapaille was well known for his research on the emotional bonds humans form with objects in their culture. Rapaille was asked to look at the problem of the Japanese not taking to coffee despite much advertising, sampling, and promotions. Then Rapaille assembled several large groups of Japanese and got them to participate in some 'stimulus experiments'. He played soothing music and got them to talk back through their earliest childhood memories which include several kinds of topics. After that, he asked them to describe their experiences with different products and what emotions they associated with them. He then asked them about their experiences with coffee, but he got no response. Most Japanese people have no memories of coffee.

They'd never tasted coffee, and hence had no emotional bond to the drink. Because in Japan they only drank tea and had been doing so for thousands of years. Coffee was a recent foreign phenomenon with no accumulated repository of memories. This was the critical insight Rapaille was looking for. He went back to the brand managers at Nestle Japan and said please don't throw endless advertising dollars in an attempt to convert the Japanese public to coffee. Your problem is much deeper.

Instead, he suggested a plan which is a longer-term strategy. He asked Nestle to focus on coffee-flavored candies and market them to Japanese children. Rapaille's plan for his research was to get the children to love Nestle's coffee flavor from an early age. This helps kids to get to know the taste of coffee and they would start to associate coffee with positive emotions.

This imprinting plan worked doubly well because Nestle, as it is, was a proven global leader in making good candy. Nestle Japan flooded the market with its coffee-flavored candies which became extremely popular with Japanese youth in no time. The secondary plan is the effect of the candy push was the filtering up of the coffee flavor to their parents, who ended up tasting the candies out of curiosity, and started to like them too.

A decade later after the perfect execution of candies, Nestle re-entered the Japanese market with a new wave of coffee offerings. This time, thankfully, the outcome would be very different. Many of their candy customers were now of working age. They were already consumers of caffeine and worked long hours. Nestle released instant baristas that were easy for home and workspaces. Instant coffee was a tremendous hit. Which says the Plan was a massive success.

Today, Nestle is the undisputed market leader in that geography. Japan today imports 500,000 tons of coffee annually. Barely 60 years earlier, it was a market that hardly sold a cup! Rapaille delivered for Nestle Japan one of the most profound case studies of modern marketing. Nestle never lost hope of giving another shot by changing plans. They changed their plans again and again and again until a plan took them to success. Of Course, the plan was perfectly executed. The flavor of green tea over rice is still a Japanese favorite. But in less than half a century, a mere couple of generations, coffee too is an integral part of the Japanese palette. Amazing isn't it. Nestle repeated the coffee plan with noodles in India. Most of India had never tasted noodles. But Maggi noodles targeted kids and won over mothers. In three decades all of India is addicted!

How amazing it will be to reach the destination after back-to-back storms on the sail. It takes nothing more than making plans, recreating plans, changing plans, and executing them perfectly.

It's not about speed, It's about direction.

In the journey to your dream, It's not about pace, it's not about progress, it's not about speed. A journey is all about the direction.

"When you are in the correct direction, don't stress over speed"

Well, when I mention speed is not important that in no way means don't care about speed. The importance of the direction must be pretty much higher than the importance of the speed. The focus plays the game in the journey. When your focus is mostly on the direction and sharing a little concentration on the pace then the journey would be cautious, but if the focus is on the speed, quick growth, and fast progress. You may miss the direction and everything could be ruined as far as you've made.

When successful people or social Influencers say through stage shows or tweets or people who personally know you use the words like Hustle - Grind - Chase, These words are misunderstood by us thinking these are speed. Speed in reaching the destination, Reaching the dream. Don't confuse speed with other words. On the journey, daily tasks or plans should be done speedily. The speed which has Perfection which has productivity. This tells you that you are on the right track and when you are on that track do not encourage any delays in daily tasks. Apply the accelerator, speed up the work and get it done.

"Speed in work, Patience in execution"

It is hard to know if you are on the right track or diverting from the track so always be more careful when shifting to other tasks. Work with speed, but execute with patience. There is a difference, work is something pretty much the same as you do it's a process of a daily or a random task, don't ever delay work. Work should be done as fast as possible because you need nothing but productivity and presence of mind to get the work done. If the work is scheduled for one hour and when you are a professional and complete the work in forty-five minutes you've just earned fifteen valuable minutes which you can use productively. Don't delay your work, in fact, reach the highest point of your speed to get the work done with productivity and perfection.

"Slow down to go faster"
-Ralph Simone

Executing, This needs a little less focus on speed but yes the track of pace is one of the major alerts. In execution, the focus should be on various things Perfection, productivity, pace and the most important is Direction. The major focus should be on the direction in the execution because no matter what you follow and how speed you maintain if that's the wrong direction, every effort is going to be wasted.

Hustle in all the work and tasks, grind and chase your dream. It's wonderful when you have the fire burning to get to your dream. Keep working hard on the plans and tasks but do not expect the destination should speedily come closer to you. Hustle as long as it takes you to your destination, do not hustle expecting your destination should speedily come closer to you.

OPINION ON LIFE

"Your opinion is your vision"

But do not of your own accord make your troubles heavier to bear and burden yourself with complaining. Pain is slight if opinion has added nothing to it; but if, on the other hand, you begin to encourage yourself and say, "It is nothing, – a trifling matter at most; keep a stout heart and it will soon cease"; then in thinking it slight, you will make it slight. Everything depends on opinion; ambition, luxury, greed, hark back to opinion. It is according to opinion that we suffer. A man is as wretched as he has convinced himself that he is.

by Lucius Annaeus Seneca the Younger. Roman philosopher

The opinion is everything, opinion is what makes you put better efforts, opinion is what makes you give up, opinion is what makes you dream big, opinion is what makes you think negative, and opinion is what makes you think positive. It could be about a person, It could be a dream, It could be a place, It could be a day, It could be an event, It could be anything. Everything in the world outside and around you depends on the opinions inside you.

There are many philosophers and successful people who have found that everything depends on opinions in one's mind. Waking up in the morning with a good opinion of the day would make your day wonderful. A heartfelt 'Good morning' wish could make your day a good day and the other person's day too. If the opinion for the day when you wake up is negative then the whole day could be negative even the good things and most awaited opportunities coming to you, your fixed opinion won't let you see them, If you start your day with 'Today is going to be an average day' Then it's going to be that way. If your opinion about today is amazing and you feel it's going to be great then you will find ways to turn your negative happenings into positive, you can turn the things around and outside you when you have a good or positive opinion inside your mind.

"Man is affected not by the events, but by the views he takes of them."
-Seneca

Opinion matters, A good opinion turns the whole bad into good, the whole negative into positive. When we have a bad opinion about a person, no matter how good he is doing to us we could never see it. Why see the bad in a good person which makes no sense. This is how blind the opinions can make you. There is nothing like having a good opinion and everything good happens. It's different. Have a good opinion and that will give you plenty of ways to turn your bad days into good.

Life, Life has many things for you and all you have to do is treasure it as much as you want. There is no limit or no end until you limit yourself and you stop wanting. Life does not know to be fair, to be unfair, to be cruel, to be wonderful. People do this but life never does it. People who are successful till now, no one ever said I got this success just because life was simple to me and gave it to me. They never said those types of statements, everyone said that they dreamed, they worked, most of them failed and again tried and finally made it. Life is never in their favor, it's equal for all. The difference between the most successful people and the ones who gave up saying life is hard on me is the 'Opinion'. Apart from all other important things which successful people went through, the beginning of everything and everyone is opinion. That is what it takes you through, gives a kick start.

"Life's not fair, Life's not unfair. It's just how you build it"

Life is never fair and life is never unfair. It's all about how you build is great, it's all about how you stopped trying to make it better, it's all about how you destroyed it. The seed of any way in life is the opinion and when you have a seed of positive opinion in you, there come plenty of hard times but this good opinion makes you see the possible ways in the hard times. And when you have a negative opinion no matter how good it is on the way and still the negative opinions can destroy all the positive comings.

Opinion involves Purpose, Purpose involves a question. If you have the purpose and the answer for that purpose then the opinion takes charge. Purpose can be anything that you wanted in your life, and for the question why is that purpose or why do you want that and the answer is whatever answer it is, I want it because it makes me happy, it makes me help others through that, it was my parents wish for me, it is my passion, it helps society, it is challenging for me, it is adventurous for me or whatever. When you want it that hard and you know what you want then you need to have an opinion on life.

Life has many new things for you every day, many surprises, many challenges, and facing all that and making it through gets you what you wanted. Life is never easy if you have an opinion that It's not easy. Life doesn't feel impossible if you have an opinion that there will be ways to turn this suffering into joy. The vision of good things coming should begin in your mind with the opinion. Don't blind yourself with the negative opinions which don't allow you to see the opportunity and the small paths to success.

I'm not talking about positive thinking, or negative thinking stuff, I'm just talking about "Opinion on life". Which is the foundation and should be carried throughout every big dream. Isn't it amazing that just having a good opinion on life keeps you charged during the whole of your journey? As an example, I would love to mention a speech from one of my favorite movies "Catch me if you can"(A true story).

"Two little mice fell in a bucket of cream. The first mouse quickly gave up and drowned. The second mouse wouldn't quit. He struggled so hard that eventually he churned that cream into butter and crawled

out. Gentlemen, as of this moment, I am that second mouse."
-Frank Abagnale

This is the speech from which we can learn a lot. The hard work, the struggle, the win. Apart from all these, mainly we are looking into something different, Both the little mice fell into the same cream. The cream is not any different for any of them. Life is just the same for everyone. The difference between both the mice is their opinion on life. Bad opinion on life blinds your vision and makes you not see the good that's coming and lets you drown. Good opinion on life gives the vision to see the ways to success through horrible situations.

Wabi-sabi, In traditional Japanese aesthetics, wabi-sabi is a world view centered on the acceptance of transience and imperfection. The aesthetic is sometimes described as one of appreciating the beauty that is "imperfect, impermanent, and incomplete" in nature. It is prevalent throughout all forms of Japanese art. As Beth Kempton mentioned in her book, Wabi Sabi, is a Japanese Wisdom for a Perfect Imperfect Life: "Put simply, wabi-sabi permits you to be yourself. It encourages you to do your best but not make yourself ill in pursuit of an unattainable goal of perfection. Wabi-sabi is all about finding beauty in imperfections and this helps them to keep a good opinion of life.

People always thrive to know the purpose of their lives, why are they born? for what? And there are few gurus who said why do humans thrive to know the purpose in fact they can just live life. But the purpose of life is nothing but what you want in this life, what you want to achieve. It could be for the whole life or just today. What makes your heart hungry is the purpose of life and that's what you need to do in life. Angela Duckworth explained Having a purpose means that, in choosing what to do, a person takes into account whether it will benefit other people. People who have this level of purpose feel a responsibility to make the world a better place and feel that their lives have meaning.

There is a theory called **Logotherapy** which was developed by neurologist and psychiatrist Viktor Frankl and is based on the premise that the primary motivational force of an individual is to find meaning in life. Frankl describes it as "the Third Viennese School of Psychotherapy" along with Freud's psychoanalysis and Adler's psychology. Frankl believed that humans are motivated by something called a **"will to meaning,"** which is the desire to find meaning in life. He argued that life can have meaning even in the most miserable of circumstances and that the motivation for living comes from finding that meaning.

Frankl argues also in this way, "the meaning of life is to be discovered in the world rather than within man or his psyche, as though it was a closed system. The meaning of life always changes, but it never ceases to be. It can be discovered in three ways according to logotherapy one, by creating a work or doing a deed. Two, by experiencing something or encountering someone. and Three, by the attitude we take toward unavoidable suffering.

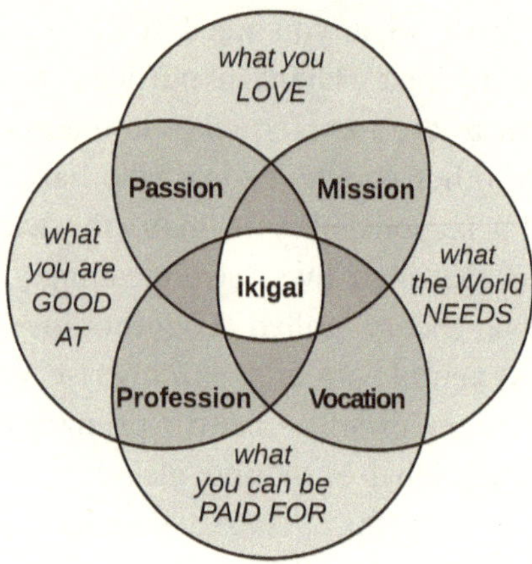

There is a very famous Japanese concept called Ikigai. Hector García and Francesc Miralles are considered the original authors of this popular concept, which was introduced in their book 'Ikigai'. Ikigai is a Japanese concept that means your 'reason for being'. ' 'Iki' in Japanese means 'life,' and 'gai' describes value or worth. Your ikigai is your purpose in life or your bliss. It's what brings you joy and inspires you to get out of bed every day. There is also a model for the concept of Ikigai which is very well explained and that helps find the purpose and bliss of living.

In this way, there are various theories and concepts introduced by different kinds of people which help humankind to keep a good opinion on life and to go after the purpose of life. Having a good Opinion on life can take you through all that you want in life. This chapter which began with an Opinion on life, explains every next step of personality which should be in sailing the storm. Having an opinion on life is the foundation of all and the major next steps to achieve your dreams are mentioned below.

GRIT

To chase the big dream in your life you should have a passion for pursuing the long-term goals which you have set for yourself. You should have grit, which means you must have the courage and show the strength of your character. A person who works hard on commitments has true grit. Grit is not a word you used to hear very often, but there is an American academic Angela Duckworth who is the founder and CEO of Character Lab, a nonprofit whose mission is to advance scientific insights that help children thrive. Angela Duckworth researched a lot and published a book called GRIT. The book mainly concentrates on Why do naturally talented people frequently fail to reach their potential while other far less gifted individuals go on to achieve amazing things? The secret to outstanding achievement is not talent, but passionate persistence.

"What we eventually accomplish may depend more on our passion and perseverance than on our innate talent"
-Angela Duckworth

Grit is very important in any walk of life and chase of dreams, the courage, the commitment and to keep working hard, practicing and making yourself a capable person in other words importantly grit is one of the major things it takes to reach your destination. Grit is a single word that combines the mixture of important qualities for sailing the storms to reach your dream.

Grit is having the courage to chase the dream with strong and barely controllable emotion and also persistence in doing something despite difficulty or delay in achieving success. It is having an idea about moving in a direction with consistency and endurance like having a clear inner compass that guides all your decisions and actions. This says a person has knowledge overall of what he is doing and the control over making the perfect decisions to be on the correct path to reach the goal. Many successful people displayed grit and reached their dreams,

Michael Jordan

He is an American former professional basketball player and businessman. Michael always loved baseball because his dad loved it so much. When he was in high school, he tried out for the varsity basketball team and did not make it because he was undersized. In the very next year, Michael grew 4 inches and he practiced relentlessly. He chased his dream ignoring all discouragements, He never allowed the thought of quitting in his mind. He made his game better every day with daily practices. Because of his amazing hard work, he averaged 25 points per game that season and the next season too. As a senior, he was selected for the McDonald's All-American team and then he achieved one of his goals: a scholarship to the University of North Carolina to play basketball. All his efforts seem to have finally rewarded him.

While at the University of North Carolina Michael focused on developing determination. Michael set his goals high in the NBA. He was selected with the third overall pick by the Chicago Bulls in 1984. He went on to win five regular-season MVP awards; six NBA championships received six NBA Finals MVP awards, three All-Star game MVP awards, and a defensive player of the year award. Michael was a man of determination, but he was most affected by his father's murder. Michael and his dad had a special bond, He loved his father so much. On July 23, 1993, Michael's life took a turn when his father, James, was murdered off Interstate 95 in North Carolina. Two locals had robbed him, shot him in the chest, and threw his body into a swamp. It took its toll on him just three months later Michael announced his retirement at age 33 from the NBA. He said, "I no longer have the desire to play." The next year Michael decided to take a different path, his father's path, and try out for baseball in the MLB. He signed a minor league contract with the Chicago White Sox in 1994. He played an unpleasant season for the Double-A Birmingham Barons.

"I've missed more than 9000 shots in my career. I've lost almost 300 games. 26 times, I've been trusted to take the game winning shot and missed. I've failed over and over and over again in my life and that is why I succeed."
~Michael Jordan

Next year Michael announced to the media "I'm back." From there on Michael would lead the Bulls to three more consecutive NBA champions and placed his name as the "NBA's greatest player of all time."

Michael Jordan stood as a man of perseverance and will to conquer, he displayed lots of grit. His goals were set high, and he was determined to reach them. Even after he was cut from his high school team, he still never gave up on his dreams. Michael Jordan displayed the grit he practiced and made him the best man and best player day by day. He never took his focus from his dream. The passion and perseverance toward his dream made him reach his destination.

Grit did not have an exact theoretical concept. Angela Duckworth with her team has defined it as. Duckworth's definition includes three key components: 1) Sustained interest, 2) Sustained effort; 3) Long-term goals.

Sustained interest: Sustaining and maintaining an interest in what you're chasing, and what you are doing, this is how excited you are about the subject after studying, same as you were when you are about to begin.

Sustained effort: Maintaining and prolonging a vigorous or determined attempt until you reach your goals or dreams.

Long-term goals: The goals that are to be accomplished in the future. Having a long vision for those goals and willing to work harder to get them.

According to Duckworth, grit is the combination of passion and perseverance which involves plenty of other components. When I was studying all about grit I found many articles, many blogs, and many sayings from various writers and successful people. The components and characteristics of grit are as follows: interest, practice, purpose, hope, courage, resolve, and strength of character. Openness, Conscientiousness, Resilience, Extroversion, Agreeableness. Determination, perfection, endurance, and a few others. After going through all that grit contains, I had a feeling that grit is like a micro storage card with a very small word that has so much stuff stored in it. Come on man be grittier is a simple word but it has a lot of stuff in it to follow or display. Well, it is hard to display grit in your chase of the dream but that's what helps you to reach the top.

Grit helps you to reach your goals because it is a driver of achievement and success. This is less about intelligence and more about all the components and characteristics mentioned above. talent may be nothing more than unmet potential. It is only with effort that talent becomes a skill that leads to success. You can increase grit by practicing.

For a big dream to be achieved the very first thing should be a good opinion on life. Then to start working and all through the journey displaying Grit would be the next thing. And in that journey when the major setbacks and breakdowns show up you will need an important part of grit, that is Resilience.

Resilience

Having the capacity to recover quickly from difficulties, toughness, and the ability to spring back into shape is the general meaning of resilience. Psychologists define resilience as the process of adapting well in the face of adversity, trauma, tragedy, setbacks, breakdowns, threats, or significant sources of stress such as relationship problems, health problems, workplace, business struggles, and financial stressors. As much as resilience involves "bouncing back" from these difficult experiences, Professor Michael Ungar gives a definition of resilience as: 'Adequate provision of health resources necessary to achieve good outcomes despite serious threats to adaptation or development.'

In very simple words Resilience is facing the tough times and finding possible ways and withstanding. Achieving something big never gets in one shot. It takes us through a lot of struggle and resilience is something very important that helps us to accept the situation and act accordingly without giving up.

Norman Garmezy

Dr. Norman Garmezy was a clinical psychologist and is often noted as being the founder of research in resilience. His research was based at the University of Minnesota in the United States of America. Garmezy defined resilience as, "not necessarily impervious to stress. Rather, resilience is designed to reflect the capacity for recovery and maintained adaptive behavior that may follow initial retreat or incapacity upon initiating a stressful event"

"Regardless of the circumstances, hard-ended resilience can carry you forward."
-Anne Finucane

Resilience is the capability of throwing ourselves back from the deepest setbacks and breakdowns. This theory is not so hard to understand, this is something everyone applies when they don't want to let go of their dream or give up on their dream when they hit the rock bottom but find the solutions and ways to get on the track, keep scaling up in all possible ways until they recover from the previous falls and stand still. To understand this concept of resilience Dr. Ginsburg developed the 7 C's model of resilience. The 7 C's are; Control, Competence, Confidence, Connection, Character, Coping, and

Contribution.

Control is most important in resilience, it could be both physical and mental, Control over-thinking process, control over decision making, and control over actions. All are equally important in tough times. Many people lack control which puts them off the track and whatever they do doesn't make any sense. And this control should be applied to other C's of resilience also.

Competence boosts your self-esteem and capabilities, That sets a spirit of developing skill and talent and being more cautious. Competence inspires and uplifts the strength and commitment towards every next step. Competency is one of the references and hope for success. It cheers you through the milestones and motivates you to learn all new skills and talents whichever is needed.

Confidence is the feeling or belief that you can have faith in or rely upon yourself to achieve the goal. Being confident keeps you holding your hope without backing off or giving up. Confidence plays a key role in the mind which gives the charge to the whole process of work. In tough times confidence is something that generates hope and helps to sail. And though confidence should be a genuine feeling that exactly shows confidence in what you can do so that it can help you to learn the skill or gain the knowledge over and get your self-confidence than that could help you in the chase.

Connection, Being connected to the atmosphere and the purpose of what you are doing where you are is important. Through the connections a lot can be learned, a lot can be foreseen, and a lot can be predicted. Pieces of Advice will be good enough when you are connected to a community of what you are going through. Connection with the goal is important, Connection with the journey makes you feel responsible. Connection with others helps you to build a sense of security.

Character, Character is what we are, and the better character comes from awareness. A set of principles personally and professionally should be followed which defines your character. To build a strong character there should be so much awareness of what is right and what is wrong. It's not only what you think is right or what you think is wrong, but awareness should also be what all people think is correct and what is not and that's when you should take your opinion on what feels correct to you and follow those opinions of yours which came from the awareness. That will be your character.

Coping is a conscious or unconscious strategy used to reduce stressful and unpleasant emotions. Coping strategies can be perceptions or behaviors and individual or social. There are various types of coping like problem-focused coping, emotion-focused coping, social support, religious coping, and meaning-making. And the coping concentrates on resilience known as problem-focused coping, emotion-focused coping, and avoidance coping. These types of coping reduce the negative impact and help you to give an active effort and response in stressful situations.

Contribution is one of the last C's, The contribution could be out of gratitude and that gratefulness defines your attitude. The contributions help you back in the way of collaborations and connections and increase the circle and that will be helpful at times you need.

Malavika Hegde

Malavika is the daughter of former Karnataka(A state in India) Chief Minister SM Krishna, she was born in 1969 in Bengaluru where she completed her schooling and her engineering from Bengaluru University. She tied the knot with VG Siddhartha in 1991.

Veerappa Gangaiah Siddhartha Hegde was an Indian businessman from Karnataka. He was the founder of the cafe chain Café Coffee Day and served as its chairman and managing director. VG Siddartha led cafe coffee day to wonderful heights. The first CCD retail outlet was launched in Bengaluru in 1996. It was meant for customers to sit and surf the internet while enjoying their coffee; hence the name 'Cafe Coffee Day. The idea of providing a place with the internet is among the innovations that set CCD on its path to emerging as the top player that it is now. In the over two decades since, CCD has become the largest coffee retailer in India with over 1,700 outlets across the country. To put that in perspective, its nearest rival, Barista, has 220 stores. Tata Starbucks has just 146 stores. CCD could achieve its low pricing point due to the fact it grows its coffee. The Chikkamagaluru-based business grows its coffee on over 20,000 acres of land and is the largest producer of Arabica coffee beans in Asia. Siddhartha himself owns a Coffee plantation spanning 12,000 acres. This is in contrast to other coffee giants that outsource their coffee. And the success of cafe coffee day has scaled up.

Later there were situations in the market that forced the stores to be closed and eventually cafe coffee day was sinking into debt. VG Siddhartha had reportedly taken the step after coming under an immense financial strain, The debt is reported to touch the mark of 11,000 crores. Siddhartha and two other CDEL directors had given personal guarantees towards loans to the tune of Rs 1,028 crore. There are stories that ran saying Siddhartha was troubled by various officials.

V.G. Siddhartha asked his driver to bring him to a bridge close to the southern city of Mangalore. Then, according to the driver, Siddhartha got out to take a walk. He was not seen again; his body recovered on the second day since he went missing.

After the death of Siddhartha, In a typewritten note released by the news agency ANI, Siddhartha founder of India's largest chain of coffee shops, Cafe Coffee Day, and a prominent early investor in the successful IT services company Mindtree Ltd. appeared to apologize for "failing to create the right profitable business model." He said pressure from his private equity partners and other lenders, as well as harassment from the various departments, had become unbearable. And yet Siddhartha wrote in his note: "My intention was never to cheat or mislead anybody, I have failed as an entrepreneur."

Then Malavika Hegde stepped up to take charge as CEO of CCD, Before becoming the CEO of Cafe Coffee Day (CCD), Malavika earlier served as a non-board member of CDEL for many years.

According to the Times of India: In a letter to the company's 25,000 employees in 2020 before Malavika took over as CEO of the company, She wrote that she was committed to the future of the company and assured that the Coffee Day story was "worth preserving". Her letter came hours after a probe revealed that a private entity owned by late founder Siddhartha owed Rs 2,693 crore to the listed entity, Coffee Day Enterprises Limited (CDEL). "We will work to reduce the debt to a manageable level by selling a few more investments as I am committed to the company's future," she wrote.

After Siddhartha's death by suicide, Malavika Hegde managed to reduce his debt even during the COVID lockdown. She made the team work with commitment as well. She mentioned the challenges have increased but "somewhere along the way, my mission has been to uphold the proud legacy of Siddhartha. He has left me a job to do, to settle every lender to the best of my ability, to grow the business, and to enthuse and foster our employees."

CDEL had a debt of INR 7000 Crore as of March 31, 2019. But as per CDEL's statement in August 2021, the management was working hard to get the firm back on track after "substantial" debt reductions. It had mentioned in its annual report that its net debt was Rs 1,731 crore as of March 31, 2021. The report read, "The total loan funds stood at Rs 1,779 crore which comprises long-term borrowings of Rs 1,263 crore and short-term borrowings of Rs 516 crore." The team brought down the debt to Rs 3,100 crore as of March 31, 2020, from Rs 7,200 crore in March 2019, without a single rupee haircut from lenders.

As a result of Malavika's initiative, Coffee Day's debt burden was reduced to Rs 1,731 crore by 2021. This is a great achievement. Malavika's goal is to make CCD a multi-billion dollar company without the debt burden. Following in the footsteps of her late husband, Malavika's dream has become to move coffee day shops to every corner of the country.

Currently, Cafe Coffee Day (CCD) owns 572 cafes across the country, along with 333 CCD Value Express kiosks. It is a huge business with over 36,000 vending machines serving coffee to CCD customers. Cafe Coffee Day (CCD), contributed 47% of the consolidated net revenue. Logistics business accounted for 45% of revenue, while the remaining 8% was from logistics.

Malavika hegde, woman of resilience. She displayed wonderful grit and stood still with hope and worked hard and she made the impossibles possible. She is the inspiration for many and the success story of CCD is now being written by Malavika Hegde. With a very good opinion of tomorrow, She showed grit and resilience in every step of her journey.

Antifragile

Antifragile is beyond resilience, The concept was developed by Nassim Nicholas Taleb, Lebanese-American essayist, mathematical statistician, former options trader, risk analyst, and aphorist whose work concerns problems of randomness, probability, and uncertainty. This concept came out to the world through his book, Antifragile, and in technical papers. Antifragility is a property of systems in which they increase in capability to thrive as a result of stressors, shocks, volatility, noise, mistakes, faults, attacks, or failures. In one word from disorders. An antifragile mindset goes far beyond practicing resilience. It is about turning turmoil into tenacity.

Taleb adds that antifragility not only enables us to face the Black Swan;(large-scale unpredictable and irregular events of massive consequences.) understanding it makes us "less intellectually fearful in accepting the role of these events as necessary for history, technology, knowledge, everything." If a fragile mindset does not like disorder, chaos, or stressors, an antifragile mindset can grow stronger through adversity. Stress can create resilience. He says that we can benefit, grow, and even thrive when we have to face some form of shocks, volatility, randomness, and disorder. When I was going through all the articles, books, and videos about antifragile I came across a ted talk "How to design antifragile systems" by Misha Kaur who is assistant commissioner, ATO Design at the Australian Taxation Office. Misha starts explaining antifragile with a small story that is so easy to understand. She says, Imagines a single candle placed on a table outside your garden, the air is still and the candle is burning steadily then the breeze sweeps across your garden and it extinguishes the flame, the candle has blown out. Now imagine the candle has been relit, but this time it's placed inside a protective lantern the breeze continues to sweep across the garden but the flame remains unaffected. However, the flame doesn't get any better. finally, Imagine you create a fire pit in your garden you bring together light kindling and logs to start the fire burning then suddenly a little disruption a little disorder the weather changes, the breeze turns into a gentle wind, the wind stokes the flames, the flames grow and spread and suddenly the fire pit roars into life bringing light and warmth into your garden. The candle was fragile; it was affected by the smallest variants of the environment when placed inside the lantern however it was made robust and unaffected but didn't get any better. In contrast to the fire pit representation of what Nassim Taleb calls anti-fragile in the case of the fire pit the flames responded to the unpredictable disorder in the weather, the wind, and the swelling leaves accelerating and intensifying the flames. With this example, Misha explained antifragile which is understandable. To be robust and resist is what resilience teaches us and anti-fragile is beyond resilience which teaches us to hit back stronger in life.

Finally, Taleb states, "the first step towards antifragility consists in first decreasing downside." As a society, we keep seeing what we can add to our lives to improve them. To make things easier, and faster, make us stronger. That seldom works. The key to a better life, to becoming antifragile, is to see what can be eliminated from your life. This is completely a different way of understanding life and dealing with tough tasks and challenges. According to Taleb, it's hard to make your life better by adding things to what you already have, the other way which is very unique is eliminating the things which you already have but are unnecessary. When you are traveling in a boat for a little far destination with all the food needed, all the set of precautionary items, all the clothes, sticks, tools and everything whichever is needed in the travel and in half way when you find there is some trouble with the boat and you found water entering into the boat then the first thing anyone does is to make the boat less weight by throwing out all stuff which is not needed or which is not important.

There is a concept called Kaizen which is a Japanese term meaning "change for the better" or "continuous improvement." It is a Japanese business philosophy regarding the processes that continuously improve operations and involve all employees. Kaizen sees improvement in productivity as a gradual and methodical process. Kaizen is an evolutionary approach calling for gradual, continuous improvement by eliminating waste. There are a few principles and elements for this concept and a big automobile company Toyota runs based on

Kaizen. This is something relatable to what Taleb said to eliminate whatever is not necessary to make your lives easy.

A good Opinion on life is what needs to dream big and to start the journey to chase your dreams and goals. Displaying grit in every step is a sign of success and showing resilience on the hardest breakdowns is very important which leads to the concept of antifragile to hit back and get on the track to success.

Make it happen

Once you are so ready and capable of sailing then all you have to do is 'Grind.' doesn't matter what will come across the way, doesn't matter how long it will take, doesn't matter how much struggle it includes. All it needs is impeccable determination and extreme focus. Well, the willpower of giving your dream as many tries as it takes. Every shot is important, opportunities are never clear to our sight or never waiting for us across the path we are heading through. Opportunities are something that will be created by the decisions we make and the plans we execute.

It's not completely about only never giving up and giving it another try, it's about the idea and the plan, it's more about correcting the previous failure of the plan and shooting another plan which is more efficient and more effective. To get a different result you need to execute a different plan. Trying the same failed plan another time is nothing but foolish.

ROVIO

Rovio Entertainment Oyj is a Finnish video game developer based in Espoo. Founded in 2003 by Helsinki University of Technology students Niklas Hed, Jarno Väkeväinen, and Kim Dikert, the company is best known for the Angry Birds franchise. Rovio is a company that has been through a lot of struggle, Rovio had 51 attempts and missed all 51. With their 52nd attempt, they made it! Rovio had its first viral hit. The company Rovio, and their billion-dollar shot is the cult classic "Angry Birds".

Former Rovio CEO Pekka Rantala summarised it this way:

"When Rovio was established in 2003, it was just a normal, very small startup, making mobile games. It was difficult for them during the first six years. They managed to bring to market more than 50 different games, but none of them were particularly successful. They were tight on resources and money; by 2009, they were close to going bankrupt. And then came this 52nd game in December 2009, and that really changed everything,

Rovio(as Relude Oy) was Founded in 2003, by a trio of Finnish university students (Niklas Hed, Jarno Väkeväinen, and Kim Dikert), the start-up was focused on doing work-for-hire stuff. However, it wasn't making any money. In 2009, the company was near bankruptcy. Because the developers at Rovio didn't give up even after their 50th failure,

During the summer, fear and pressure were building within everyone in the company, one of the company's designers Jaakko Iisalo came up with a rough drawing. He created a simple screenshot of an angry-looking bird and showed it to his coworkers. All the team loved the character. The chief marketing officer and CEO in the room also liked the character very well. They do not know anything about the game mechanics or what type of game they are going to design with that character. All they knew is we had great character and we should execute the new plan.

CEO Pekka Rantala says, "The iPhone opened up the whole world. You had one contact, plus worldwide distribution. If we succeed there, we can go to other smartphones. And if we do well there, we can go to PC and console, and beyond. We planned this out well ahead of Angry Birds."

The team completely focused on developing games on that character for Apple's new App Store. They knew that they had the potential product in their hands and they wanted to conquer the app store first. The whole team worked so hard in developing the story which gives reason for the birds to be angry and the design of the character development. After a lot of effort and work, Angry Birds was launched in the App store.

In the early results, angry birds didn't get any traction in big markets like the UK and US, but the guys did stir up the show in their native Finland, and the game did well in Finland. The bad tractions scared the team that they were going to have another failure on their hands, so the Rovio team decided to change their strategy. They started focusing on the smaller markets first. The game got a hike in Sweden when a local skiing star mentioned in an interview that she uses the game to relax in her free time. And a few other small countries followed it too. This produced some good traction. However, it was still struggling in the big money markets "Angry Birds" became featured as the game of the week. Immediately, it went to the number 1 spot in the UK. and it reached the same position in the US several months later. This is how the success journey began for Rovio.

51 Failed attempts and still the desire was burning within all the people in the company and besides the pressure, all the team Rovio could focus on the new plans and perfect executions. It is just amazing how they achieved the success that they deserve after all the hard work and determination. They had the grit, displayed resilience, and also applied antifragile which combinedly made it happen.

There are many other companies and products which have turned from a sinking situation to massive success. All it needs is another better plan with perfect execution. And you can make it happen too.

Opinion on Life

A good opinion on life matters and that is what makes you dream big and take you to reach your destination. Bad days will always hit every once in a while sometimes it's not just days it could be a phase of a certain time frame. Just not bad but at times it could be worse too but that too shall pass with the way you respond to it and deal with it. Bad days in work-life or bad days in personal life are just like hiccups in between a stage talk or a speech. 5 or 10 secs of Hiccup cannot ruin your 30 mins speech. If you have the hiccups between the speech you will overcome them very quickly in a maximum of 3 secs and you don't just go with the flow which you had before but you will put extra effort to get the attention of the audience. The same way of response is needed for the bad days and bad times.

"Bad days are like hiccups in between the speech"

Never give a pause at the bad times and wait for the time to turn around or the favor to be on your side and then you will work again, no it doesn't work that way. For the favor to be on your side you should make it happen, The way you deal with the situation is all it needs.

It could be a bad day, It could be a good day both have the same time frame. Good times will pass and bad times will pass too. But what's important is at this moment what you are doing is what results in your next moment. The rewards are always according to what you did previously. Every hard work will pay you off, and every time of struggle will pass. Time is never still, time keeps running no matter what. The good opinion of life will make it happen no matter how big is your dream and no matter what the odds are against you. Just keep working, never stop at bad times cause time never pauses. Life goes on.

SET OF PRINCIPLES

"Principles are pillars"

Principles are the propositions or values that will act as the guide for behavior or evaluation. Multiple values and morals are called principles and that is called the character of someone who follows them.

Principles are supposed to be formed by opinions. When you have certain opinions on life, personal and professional, and when you start climbing the mountain of your dreams based on those opinions you should have a set of principles for both personal and professional. Achieving a big dream or a goal will not earn you money, position, respect, assets, or whatever it may be. Achieving your ambition makes you a way different person. The journey of success is the process of an individual to change, correct a lot and be a completely different person. And the character of that person you become gets you all the respect, money, capabilities, assets, and every little thing you ever wanted.

"Change your opinions, Keep to your principles; change your leaves, Keep intact to your roots."
-Victor Hugo

The change in a person or the change in self should be by the principles which are set by the opinions. Principles are what you are, They tell you how to react at times, and what decision should be made, The clear vision of the situation comes with the strong principles. Principles can be formed slowly. It could be a very small principle but it has to be clear what you are going to do in those types of situations. What you don't know doesn't need to have the principle yet until you gain knowledge over it and let your opinion set you the principle. What you believe today could change tomorrow and there are many open ways for your opinions to split and shuffle as the things change in the world and people change with time. No matter how many times your opinions keep changing based on the change of time but principles are never flexible. Principles are the pillars of character. To explain it easily with a very small and understandable example, when I travel in a car with few other people of my family and friends, When our car is at the signal waiting in traffic there comes beggars who are not old, don't seem physically or mentally ill, but yes lean and messy. Few people in my car have an opinion that those types of beggars are lazy to earn their bread which they are capable of working as they seem very fine so as their principle these people don't offer any money for those types of beggars. And few other people just give the money little or more to any beggar. In their opinion, they feel no one knows what illness that beggar is going through or the situation would be tough on him and their principle says to give money to help that beggar. And few other people are also there whose principle is to give money because in their opinion when they give money then they get money.

In this way, there are different types of opinions that form an individual's principles. and opinions on that particular beggar may change or opinions can change for every other beggar but the principle of the individual will never change. Principles are like a blueprint of what you are, and how you're going to handle the situations. And the rules which you set for yourself and walk on them.

Every successful person by the time they reach their goal will have a set of principles and as we see in society every time people seek advice from successful people they will be asking what are the key principles that made you succeed, what are the principles you follow and such things. Because principles are set in ourselves depending upon our ambition and making decisions according to those principles will move us a step ahead in our journey. When we have a goal or a dream which is big, at that particular moment itself we need to have a few general principles which help us in chasing the dream. For instance, if your goal is to be an athlete then the immediate principle you should have is to practice at least 2 hours a day, eat healthy food to maintain fitness, and if your goal is to be a doctor you will in general have to make a certain time frame every day to study the subject. In this way when you have the principles which are set by your opinions according to your goals, This helps you to climb to the peak.

Principles that are personal will make a difference in your profession, And principles that are professional will make changes in your personal life. There is no way that principles in different areas are not related. In any area, professional or personal, every principle affects all your life. Those principles you set and follow are your lifestyle and the rewards, results, and consequences are going to be based on the principles of your life.

"Acquire the principles and build yourself, those principles will earn you everything."

Few of the Ultimate purposes of our dreams are to make good money, earn respect, and be satisfied. Your journey does not earn you respect, your journey doesn't get you money. The journey makes you a completely different person who has a strong character of principles and is most capable of climbing the toughest mountains and worthy of the sweetest success. And that character which was built on the principles will get you to respect in society, and that capabilities which you earned will make you money, And the sweetest success gets you satisfaction.

"An army of principles can penetrate, where an army of soldiers cannot."-Thomas Paine

Success is built differently, it is less about just working hard and nothing else and more about working on the principles with an exact purpose and in the consciousness of happenings. Principles are very important for any individual or group of people to reach something big. It tends to keep you on the path of discipline and determination. Sometimes in personal life and professional life, we already have a few principles as default but those are not strong enough as we do not consider them as principles but just habits.

My brother says he never drives into a wrong route no matter what and that is not just out of respect towards traffic rules but for his safety, he is known as the man who never drives into the wrong route no matter what, in my family, everyone thinks it is one of the principles he has but he never considered it as the principle and that is the reason he very rarely drives into the wrong route and gives a reason that situation demanded so I did, of course, he feels very bad about himself driving into the wrong route but still he does that because he did not consider it as the strong principle. This is how we confuse habits with principles, Habits are flexible but principles are never flexible.

A friend of mine met with a road accident with minor wounds and his chin was deeply cut and few scratches over the face and head, he wears a helmet all the time and his mother said it was late night and he said there is no traffic so he didn't take helmet that time and he met with an accident. These are the exact situations where your principles help you and these are inevitable cause you don't know what damage would happen if you don't follow the principle but when you do something standing off the principle and then you will see things falling off.

Wearing a helmet, No smoking, Limited drinks at a party, Early morning wakeup and sleep on time, etc... There are many principles like this that seem so small but these reflect major rewards in life.

Think possibly

Thinking is what makes all the difference, everything starts with Thinking, and the thinking keeps on going and everything will be turned around, everything will be amazingly great or everything could be unbelievably depressing. How you can think and how you keep thinking inside your head creates the world outside for you. We have been taught to think positively, all of us have been raised with the same concept of thinking positively which I found to be a glitch. Yes, thinking positive is a real deception in the world of chasing real dreams. Thinking positively has to be replaced to see better rewards. The mindset should be positive, Vibe should be positive, and we should execute plans with a positive attitude. But thinking should be never only positive. Thinking only positively is deception. Replace positive thinking with possibility thinking.

Thinking is very powerful and generates millions of questions and plenty of solutions when we are thinking and that glorious process will simply be withered if we think it is all positive but not what is possible. We are making it one-sided thinking, we are thinking in our favor, and calling it positive thinking is a pure deception.

Elon musk says

"One of the biggest mistakes people usually make and feel guilty about it too, is wishful thinking.You want something to be true even if it isn't true. So you ignore the real truth for what you want to be true, This is a very

difficult trap to avoid. But if you just take that approach you're always to some degree wrong and your goal is to be less wrong. And solicit critical feedback particularly from friends. If somebody loves you they want the best for you. They don't want to tell you the bad things, so you have to ask them. I really do want to know and they will tell you."

The above brief by Elon musk is a real game-changer for me in the early steps of my entrepreneurial journey. And I realized the actual difference between positive thinking and possible thinking when I started putting my ideas into reality and my plans into execution. and everything which is resulting now has a beginning and that beginning is the thinking in our minds.

Positive thinking is to think about everything in the way we want them to happen, no matter what barriers are in our way our positive thinking can easily blind us from seeing those barriers and bushes. If thinking positively helps then every athlete who says he is pretty sure he will win this race should win but we often find plenty of videos of interviews where those who give the positive statements about the game, race, or whatever end up losing against the one who was calm and doesn't give as positive statements as the opponent gives. Positive thinking can lead one to overconfidence which changes the complete game. Positive thinking could be very bad as we lose our vision over the truth and we just keep ourselves in the illusion of a positive situation, which is a clear trap.

Possible thinking, This type of thinking is something needed for everyone in general but keenly for the 2% of people who are looking to achieve a lot and start chasing their dreams or who are about to start the run towards their goals. This is a game about the presence of mind and a fair way of thinking to achieve bigger things. Possible thinking is to think genuinely and Honestly. This process of thinking raises correct questions as you are thinking and the solutions are also to be run in your mind considering all the odds. This process enlightens you and makes the vision very clear on how hard is this going to be and what are the best ways to choose, what are the decisions which have to be taken, and how you should prepare yourself to face the coming tough times and that is when you work on what you need to develop within your capabilities that should make you more strong and ready to get the work done.

Thinking should always be on possibilities, think possible but not positive, On the chase towards the milestones and the goals we should be pretty much optimistic. There are a lot of differences between being optimistic, having a positive attitude, Creating a positive work atmosphere, and Adapting positive intentions and positive thinking. Positive thinking is in no way related to all others. One who wants success should be optimistic and with a completely positive attitude and mindset while thinking possibly. Every characteristic should be positive but thinking should not be positive but possibly.

WOOP

Princess Gabriele of Oettingen-Oettingen and Oettingen-Spielberg, known professionally as Gabriele Oettingen, is a German academic and psychologist. She is a professor of psychology at New York University and the University of Hamburg. Oettingen is the Scientist who explained why positive thinking can be bad for Your health. It can make you less likely to get things done. Oettingen spent 20 years researching positive thinking, she concludes positive thinking can be counterproductive.

According to Oettingen, staying positive might be bad for you. In the short term, it may feel better while imagining achieving the goals but in the long term it leads to inaction, underperformance, and less likely to achieve the goals. Oettingen and her team researched people from different countries about personal health, academic, professional, and relationship goals.

After research among students about their crush, Oettingen concluded "We achieve our goals virtually and thus feel less need to take action in the real world."As people imagine everything that they want to come true, they have already virtually achieved that in their thinking and imaginations and that takes off all the power which should be in efforts for making it happen in real life. So positive thinking gives satisfaction in the short term as people just think positively the odds are in their favor and later in the long run it leads to depression and failure.

Oettingen with her team asked a few people to think positively about a challenge, then focus on the largest blocks preventing them from overcoming the challenge and write down their thoughts. Two weeks later she reports that people who considered the obstacles and positive overcomes from those barriers are more successful than the people who didn't even care about the obstacles.

Oettingen and the team came up with a formulation called **WOOP**, which means Wish, Outcome, Obstacle, Plan. Oettingen suggested the process of four steps to follow in tough times.

Wish: Visualise what you want to happen

Outcome: Visualise the implications of the "wish" coming true

Obstacle: Figure out what's preventing it from coming true

Plan: Figure out what you will do next time you're faced with the obstacle

You must ask

What is it in me that stands in the way of my imagined positive outcome ?

What's my inner obstacle ?

-Dr. Gabriele Oettingen

Ottingen says this has been shown to work for people who are depressed, This four-step process is the exact way of thinking possibly. The possibilities of happening, The possibilities of all obstacles, and all the possibilities of overcoming them. This way of thinking is called possibility thinking.

POSSIBILITIES

Why should you think of possibilities? This should be the question to get to know this in detail. Thinking of what we wish is pretty much simply because we can just go on to think about whatever we wish. But thinking of possible happenings, thinking of possible obstacles, and thinking of overcoming those obstacles are not easy at any time. This thinking needs a lot of focus and seriousness, during this process the one who is thinking will undergo many emotions like fear, anxiety, depression, and dullness but in the end, when they find the possible ways to make their dream come true that will be the sweetest moment and at that point of time they knew they have to put efforts like crazy to make it happen and as they already have an idea of what hindrances are about to come so they will work hard with great cautiousness and lot more focus and achieve the goal.

It's all about possibilities and what we decide, our decisions take us to possible ways only. And those could be possible ways for failures and possible ways for success. What we analyze before making a move depending on the possibilities leads us accordingly. We all know Rubik's cube puzzle toy, The Rubik's Cube is an iconic puzzle toy. But it is mathematically complicated, there are 43 quintillion possible configurations of the Cube. Over 30 years after the Cube was invented, a group of mathematicians showed, using a bank of supercomputers at Google, that any cube could be solved in at most 20 moves only. The original 3x3x3 Rubik's cube has 43 252 003 274 489 856 000 combinations of possibilities to be solved but also it is always only 20 possible moves away to be solved. Most of the time we are very close to the destination but just because we don't think of possibilities beforehand we will be delayed. That is why thinking of possibilities is very important.

Murphy's law

Why will people always ask to think positively? Even successful people always suggest thinking positively and nothing else. Parents, teachers, and mentors no matter who and no matter what situation someone is in, everyone around the globe always tells them to think positive and everything falls in place. Why is that? Why do people believe thinking positive is so much more important than any other thing? When successful people suggest thinking positive that doesn't mean getting into a comfort zone of relaxing and thinking everything according to you and everything which pleases you. That suggestion is to be optimistic, never be negative even for a while, and never be negative. Being positive in tough situations lets your brain work sharply with less stress, which is very helpful to overcome those types of tough situations.

There is an idiom **'Never say never'** used to explain that nothing is impossible and anything can happen. This expression was first recorded in Charles Dickens's Pickwick Papers (1837). There are many people who said many times to never say never Because anything can happen with the efforts there is nothing ever fixed that this will never happen and you can't do this.

"Never say never, because limits like fear are often just an illusion."
- Micheal jordan

Just as Jordan stated many other people also did state never to say never, But why? Why shouldn't we say never? Why should we be optimistic? Why should we try to create positive energy? Why do all successful people keep saying these? Because There is negative energy and negative force in saying never and not being positive. Yes, it's true not being optimistic may not let the positive things go. Being negative with words like never may let negative things happen.

There is an important law called **Murphy's Law,** Murphy's law is an adage or epigram that is typically stated as: *"Anything that can go wrong will go wrong."* This Law is usually attributed to Captain Edward Murphy, who served at Edwards Air Force base in 1949. Murphy's law is not about pessimism. If you are prepared that anything that can go wrong will go wrong. The tendency to think that everything that can go wrong, will go wrong is a cognitive bias called Murphy's Law. Stress and mood are two crucial elements that play a role in shaping the cognitions of this bias. A cognitive bias is a systematic pattern of deviation from norm or rationality in judgment. Individuals create their own "subjective reality" from their perception of the input.

This law was evidently proven by many other researchers with many examples. Murphy's law is very simple to understand as this law involves many elements, few are easy to understand and few are hard to accept which makes it tough to understand. But the basic track of the law is the more we think or imagine something bad or wrong happening the more it will happen. This is simply because we experience it in the daily routine of our life. To explain it more thoroughly, one of the common situations is misplacing or forgetting things. We keep telling ourselves that I always lose stuff and maybe I'll forget or misplace this item and that will happen. While cooking or holding something or doing something important you keep telling yourself I think I may have used more salt, I'm scared I may slip this thing from my hand, I think I did this work in a wrong way, and yes it turns out to be wrong. It seems we have experienced this and been experiencing it in our daily life. The same applies to all small to big situations.

This is the reason people who have been through the success journey will always suggest we be optimistic. And the saying 'Never to say Never' is very important for all the reasons explained in the law. This is hard to follow when we don't understand this process and it is very easy to understand when we could understand and adapt it. Thinking is the beginning of everything and if it is correct everything will fall in place at some point in time but if it is not correct everything will fall apart.

Imagination

There is a major misunderstanding about 'Think positive' people often confuse thinking positive with imagining positive, we could also eliminate the word positive and say the confusion is in between thinking and imagining. Imagination is very powerful, imagination is completely different from thinking. Imagination should be very positive and it is just whatever we want to happen but thinking is a different game it is about possibilities and more practical.

Steve Harvey says,

You should dream outlandish dreams, if it's in your imagination, it is possible. Do you know you can't imagine something that can't happen? You know it's impossible to think of the impossible? It's not possible. So if you think about it, it's possible. And if you live your life in possibilities instead of probabilities you have a great chance of finding happiness. Never live your life in a probability, there is a statistics of tracks attached to a probability. A possibility has no statistics attached to it. Live your life in possibility and you'll change everything. Just change the way you think. This is really the science of becoming successful. It's simply how you think, if you change your thoughts You will change your attitude, you will change your altitude. That's all. Its law of attraction.

Steve conveys the importance of thinking, Possibility thinking and the power of imagination. Imagining is very powerful. Dreams come from imagination no matter how big you want to imagine you can imagine. Never be scared to imagine impossible things and to dream big.

> **"History has proven that those who dare to imagine the impossible are the ones who break all the limitations."**
> **-Abdul kalam**

Imagine the impossibles, dream big. But in the journey to the goals don't drown in the deception of positive thinking. Thinking is supposed to be about possibilities. The moves, the barriers, the solutions, the executions, and the results would speak.

DEINMO

In the beginning days of my entrepreneurial journey, I am so clear and confident about many things which are involved in the journey and once I started my ride towards my dream then I came to know that everything I'm confident about and everything I thought I know is something I never knew. This chasing bigger dream needs a lot more things involved, a lot more clarity, a lot more observation, and a lot more learning. Then I took my time in understanding things and learning the gaps between small confusions we all have and we never knew them.

The day I started to work on a startup is the day I opened my mind to the world and started seeing the real world. Until then what I thought the world was, then is a completely different one. I very soon came to know That I have to know so many things and learn so many things. I started learning instead of reading, Started watching and observing instead of looking, many analyses, and realizations came on the way and every single day working on my startup I'm aware of many things which I have practically executed, stood still, came up with new plans, corrections, facing rejections, dominations, every little thing made me learn big lessons and made me a more capable person for next task.

After I began my journey a few months passed and then there was small research I've made and found a small glitch that is resulting in big changes in the lives of people who are running towards their goals no matter small or big ones. For every student, employee, manager, businessman, or whoever it may be, in the present running world, the majority of people are working on a purpose, looking towards their goals. And everyone is trying to learn the things which will help them to succeed but there comes the confusion with understanding and executing what they learned from whatever article, news, books, or social media videos.

Every person who has a dream to achieve will be knowing these three powerful words. Motivation, Determination, and Inspiration. These words are very powerful but in present times we actually could not see the ultimate power behind these words because they are used very often by a lot of people now and then. The confusion among these words is in understanding and not knowing when to apply what. All three are different and have their side of power and strength which helps in the chase of any dream or goal.

In my survey when I asked different kinds of people about the meanings of these words, almost every individual gave the perfect answers. And then as my next question when I explained to them a situation and asked them what are you going to apply in these three words to overcome those situations majority of people failed to get it correct. That's where I find the confusion in people about not knowing how and when to use those powers.

Then I came up with the concept '**DEINMO**' This word is the mixture of all three powerful words *Determination, Inspiration, and motivation.* The combination of these three powers is 'Deinmo' which is the ultimate power that will act as the fuel for the chase of dreams and goals. Well, the most important part of this concept is to know when to use what. It is very simple to understand, all you have to know is what exactly happened, what exactly you are doing, and what exactly you want. As simple as it is.

Motivation

Motivation is the mental energy which helps you to initiate the work for the commitments you've made and to achieve your goals. This motivation has a little life span like a matchstick. With that fire before the match stick extinguishes we should use it to light. Motivation is important at many times, to start a big work, or a small task, or to rework, to start a day, or an extra hour. Many times in work we will need motivation to give a push.

Daniel Goleman is an author and science journalist. For twelve years, he wrote for The New York Times, reporting on the brain and behavioural sciences. Goleman identified four elements that make up motivation, Personal drive to achieve which is the desire to improve or to meet certain standards; Commitment to personal or organisational goals; Initiative which he defined as 'readiness to act on opportunities'; and Optimism which is the ability to keep going and pursue goals in the phase of setbacks. This is also known as resilience.

Motivation is really more helpful when it begins within you, getting motivated by the speeches all the time is not upto the mark for people who are chasing a big dream, Searching for motivation is not the exact thinking for a person who has big goals. Getting motivated by speeches or extracting the motivation from the stories is real good stuff but searching for them because they will keep us to work is not right. When you have the burning desire towards your goal, you will need no other motivation but just your dream. Looking at the dream which is far away makes you get to work at present. Motivation should start within you from the burning desire you have towards your dream.

Your dream should be your motivation every morning, every extra hour, every set back and every drop. And the speeches or stories from motivational videos should give you optimism, give the strength to the motivation you had within you. Self motivation is real helping power. Goleman explains that there are two types of motivation: Intrinsic and Extrinsic. Intrinsic is related to what we want to do, Extrinsic is related to what you have to do. And self motivation is not so easy to develop. It really needs the hunger to succeed and focus towards the dream and that could give you enough motivation in the stressful times and struggle.

Determination

Determination is a positive emotional feeling that involves persevering toward a difficult goal despite obstacles. Determination occurs before goal attainment and serves to motivate behavior that will help achieve one's goal. Determination is the emotion that should be from the beginning of the journey to the end constantly. Being determined is all anyone will ever need to fulfill the dream or achieve the goal. From the time when the plan is started in one's mind and from that moment determination should take place and continue till the very end of the amazing success ride.

Determination is the consistency of motivation, it is to be motivated all the time, life span of determination is like eternal fire. This is constant power throughout the whole journey. Once your mind starts to believe in your idea then determination is the power that will make you stand still, get up when you have a fall, hit back when you have to, extra effort every single time. Being determined is the constant power that reflects hope, optimism, satisfaction with what you are doing, responsibility and many other things will be included.

Determination is not something that can be adapted. Unlike motivation and inspiration, this determination will have to develop within you depending upon how badly you have the desire to succeed and to achieve the goal. All these make you a determined person and this determination is an amazing power of consistency that never lets you go off the focus.

In psychology, a determination is a very important concept that refers to the individual's ability to make choices in their lives. Self-determination implies complete control over decisions, situations, and life. Determination is about hope or knowing what they are doing has had a positive outcome at a certain point in time. And this impacts motivation. People will be more motivated with self-determination. Research recommends that having self-determination fosters success in life.

There is a theory for self-determination which is developed by psychologists Edward Deci and Richard Ryan, who first introduced their ideas in their 1985 book Self-Determination and Intrinsic Motivation in Human Behaviour. This theory suggests that people can become self-determined when their needs for competence, connection, and autonomy are fulfilled. And there are two key assumptions of the theory: The need for growth drives behavior and Autonomous motivation is important. The first assumption of self-determination theory is that people are actively directed toward growth. And the second assumption is that people are often motivated to act by external rewards.

So this self-determination is to be in complete control of emotions and be the master of the situations, and decisions, and manage every step in the correct and confident manner in the whole process of the journey.

Determination is the consistent power in a complete journey.

Inspiration

Inspiration is the divine influence, says Theology. Inspiration shows a huge effect on an individual in tough times. Inspiration is the power that spikes up the fighting spirit and builds the never give up attitude. One can be inspired by various things, Could be a biography, could be from the success of an organization or an individual, could be from someone's fighting spirit, could be from someone's failure or past failure an individual and so many other aspects. There are so many successful people, and success stories to inspire.

There is no direct definition for the word inspiration. It is a complex emotion, one that dives into the human mind and quantifies our feelings, affecting us in a unique way. Perhaps it connects with our life experiences. Whatever the reason, inspiration does not limit its possibilities. Inspiration is often used to motivate people who are working on something on purpose, chasing a dream, But the impact of inspiration is more than just in our professional lives but also in our personal lives in many situations. To be inspired is to find a moment in time that transcends that of its present and becomes a part of our lives.

Inspiration is like a bonfire once it starts to light and the more bad wind blows the brighter it fires. Inspiration mostly takes a stand in the worst situations, and the worse or tough the situations get the better inspiration shows effect. This inspiration is the power that helps all the time but mostly it takes real charge when everything's falling apart. To not get low, to not give up, to hit back.

The combination of these three powers is the ultimate power 'DEINMO' This is fuel for the journey to success. Achieving your dreams and goals will have more possibilities when you have this power within you. The clarity of when to use which power is very important. As part of my research, I have put a few situations with different aged people, and most youngsters have said all they need is motivation in any kind of situation, for the question what should you apply primarily and what should be constant when there is a huge setback or a break down in the journey, most youngsters said we need motivation and determination at few times. But in the major failures one should have the power of inspiration to stand still and get back with a new plan and that inspiration could be from anyone or from past failure itself that helps to not just repeat the process once again which is dumb but this power helps to hit back better and more capable and to start executing, then comes motivation and where the determination is a constant power through the journey.

Self-motivation to start every little task in the big journey, burning desire that helps to be determined in all hard times through the journey, and being inspired to rise from the major failures and hit back better. Hold this ultimate power 'DEINMO' with you and reach the peak stairs of success.

GAP BETWEEN ADVICE AND IGNORANCE

"Ignorance, The root and stem of down-fall"

Advice is often expected by people who are on the road to their dreams, also by the employees who are looking for a promotion or at any critical work error. Advice is important and is expected from every single person in whatever they are doing. And strangely, everyone seeks advice, and the ones who are lucky to get advice are the ones who ignore them, Right at that moment. Well, I've ignored the pieces of advice in the beginning and that is something a very precious lesson I feel I'm blessed to learn that advice is not to ignore, in the very early stage of my career and I started to respect the advice from then on no matter who is the other person advised me or just suggest me something.

Francesca Gino is an Italian-American behavioral scientist and the Tandon Family Professor of Business

Administration and unit head of the Negotiation, Organisations, and Markets unit at the Harvard Business School. Francesca Gino has found that despite evidence from many studies our decisions greatly benefit from another pair of eyes, we simply obstruct ourselves by refusing to take advice. Gino gave the reasons why people don't take the advice based on the study.

In one study, Gino and her colleagues Leigh Plunkett Tost and Richard Larrick discovered that making people feel powerful even temporarily. by asking them to describe a time when they had control over others significantly reduced their willingness to use advice. Taking advice somehow feels like admitting that they don't deserve their high status. According to another series of experiments, Gino and her colleagues found that if you're feeling anxious you will probably take that advice.

Most of the time we ignore taking advice is because we think we are smarter than the person who is advising us, or the person who advised will get the credit in the first place, or we think we are in a completely different situation than the person who is advising was been into, so this is not correct one to take advice from. We simply strike off the advice without even giving it thought just because of a feeling I'm smarter or the other person doesn't understand what I am doing.

There came a point in my life when I came to know that advice is not to be ignored without a keen understanding of it because the other pair of eyes seeing us doing something can actually see that we are taking a negative diversion which we can't realize by ourselves. One fine day a sister of mine who is working for a corporate company called me ànd said, Danny! There is an opportunity to earn money online by spending like 15 mins every day. The respective company is paying so many people who are completing the given tasks which takes very less time to spare and it's easy earning so you also join the company. I didn't care about that earning thing but after a week I saw her earning money daily and saw that money credited to the account. Then again she asked me to join with her referral for which she will get some referral money and I would get a subsidy according to the company terms. Then I and my guys asked for all the details of the company and we started digging about the company and the task process and every little thing. Yes, we wanted to be smart. We have gone through everything. The name of the company is Tasman which is operating from the UK(mentioned on the respective website) so we have gone through every corner of the internet exploring about the company and known every little thing which showed no clear information and also everything is suspicious. Then we looked at the work process. To join the company, employees should pay the entry amount, there are various plans for low to high fees for respective positions. And the work process is There will be a few social media platforms that will be displayed and we should select one of them and we should hit like and subscribe to the provided accounts and capture a screenshot and upload it to the dashboard given is the work process for which we will get paid for each task like that. So simple isn't it. When we see earning is this simple that implies it is a **scam**. And the payments as so-called salaries will be added to the wallet and we should be able to withdraw them to our bank account concerning terms and conditions.

We guys concluded that it is a pure scam. But we saw many people getting money every single day for doing nothing and we also knew this process would go on for a while until the company gets enough deposits. Then we started studying between lines about the company when exactly they got their first few customers and how they operated the system and everything. There are a few social media groups in which every employee is a member and all the information will be shared there. A rough history by the time we saw about the company is that the company started 2 months ago, there are 17000 people joined, and earning money every day and new deposits are being deposited every single day. Then we estimated what would be his investment and the target amount he wanted to get from the people and what could be his estimated time. For all these, we made clear that he is brilliantly executing the scam by tempting people by showing subsidies and all. He has a very good website which is handling the traffic 24/7 and the transactions, deposits, uploads everything is excellently being executed. So putting everything in our mind being extremely smarter than the person who is running the scam we decided what his plans are and what they must be, he will need at least 3 months for the 'X' amount of money we thought would be his targeted amount based on the investment we have calculated. So we are so sure about the numbers we have made and we wanted to invest our money in it for which we will be getting back our money with 5 times more in just 1 month. We are pretty excited that we are going to scam the scammer, how smart are we? I have explained everything to the elders in our homes to get the investment money which is more money to invest for a middle-class family. Well the other pair of eyes, Told us 'NO' what you are doing ends badly. Don't be foolish, this doesn't work how you wanted it to work. We being the smartest people replied you don't get this stuff let us do what we are doing. We ignored the advice then and there. Without hesitation.

Of Course, we proceeded to invest, and in exactly 9 days the company turned down. The craziest thing is that 17000 people became 30000 in just 9 days. We have drowned in disappointment. We know the same is going to happen but we tried to be over smart for which we are really lucky we've been advised. But we were so foolish that we didn't even give a thought to the advice at least once. A great lesson for me. Expensive too. As we spent a pretty much money on that lesson and a lot of consequences because of what we did, I'm never going to forget that lesson in my life. This is when I started respecting advice.

"Fill the gap between receiving advice and ignoring it with 'Thinking'."

The response to a piece of advice never needs to be Acceptance, But it should not be ignored. There should be a gap between advice and ignorance. That gap should be filled by Realising, analyzing, and rethinking. After that just go for whatever instinct tells you, it doesn't matter. But for sure there should be a gap and that will definitely be enlightenment. The feeling which makes me less intelligent if the person who advised found me at least thinking about his advice is what makes us ignore the advice real quick and that response is something that takes everything in a wrong direction. There is something really important I have learned in a coffee shop. It took me 13 minutes to learn a lesson that will forever make me a better person to see the world differently.

My friend and I are on a business trip and we have a meeting the next morning and we've prepared everything and the time was almost 11.30 PM and both of us were tired of all the work and we badly need to drink something hot and to have something a little bit before we sleep. So we walked out of our hotel room at midnight and found a cafe named The Chocolate room within walkable distance and we entered the cafe. We ordered something to eat and my friend picked something to drink for himself and I took the menu to choose and I just simply wanted to go for whichever is low in fare. The first one I saw in hot beverages is Espresso, then the game began. I simply said okay I'll have espresso to the waiter, the waiter took a pause. And said, sir, espresso is very strong coffee it will not be comfortable to drink. Would you like to change the order? Then my mind is processing so fast that if I say Okay let me change, or okay I don't know that it is a strong coffee and all these then the waiter thinks I don't know that espresso is a strong coffee. And in a split second, I responded No don't change I'll have espresso thank you. In just 10 mins I tasted espresso and the waiter caught my expression while I tasted it. I couldn't sip another time. It's hell bitter. Then I tried to act normal and keep sipping the espresso but I really couldn't. At that point, I said to myself no I can't fake it anymore and I stopped. Before we received the bill I realized a very important thing, The waiter who advised me is working in the cafe and there is no way that I will have greater knowledge of coffees than the man who works there. Just 10 mins back when the waiter advised me not to choose espresso, how would it be if I didn't respond in ignorance but if I have taken a pause, and said okay suggest something good which comes at a low fare. I would have enjoyed a really good coffee. Or if not that, I would have also asked him what you mean by espresso is a strong coffee and he would give an explanation, there will be no milk and all so I would have picked something else and I would have still got something good to drink.

That day I knew, that stopping at the advice and analyzing it or knowing more about it doesn't make us any less intelligent or less smart. When we go to a new place or do something new it will help-seeking advice from people who are experienced or from people who have knowledge over that stuff. Advice is not to be ignored. It is to be Realised, analyzed, and rethinked.

"Don't change, Correct."

Being successful is not about money, respect, fame, or assets. It's about becoming a completely different person. A person who is entirely different from when you begin the journey to reach the destination. Change is what everyone asks you, the world expects change from you to grow in every small and big race. Every human being is unlike the other. No people are the same in this world. When you have your character which says what you are, how can you lose it by changing and acting like someone else? So when the world asks you for a change if you look into it it's not exactly the change, it's asking something which you need to correct in yourself and that's it. Correcting yourself in every little thing to make you better every day for every small progress in life.

"You are a Masterpiece. Don't change yourself, keep correcting yourself."

To achieve something big you need to be a capable person to make it through and to be a capable person all you have to do is correct yourself, every habit which should be corrected, the way you think should be corrected, the way you talk should be corrected, the way you listen and read should be corrected, the way you spend money, the way you eat, behave, every little thing in life should be corrected until it gets productive, it gets quality. Never lose yourself because no one can ever change and stay as a changed person for so long. Change is not permanent, corrections whatever you will make to yourself will make you a different person and that will be permanent because you are not changing yourself, you are building yourself. Growth is different from change. Grow yourself by correcting everything within you which needs to be corrected.

"To be yourself in a world that is constantly trying to make you something else is the greatest accomplishment."
-Ralph Waldo Emerson

Ralph said exactly. The world always wants you to change, the people always want you to change. Your friends want you to be one way, your parents want you to be another way, your partner wants you to be another way, and so does your boss. Everyone wants you to change, every phase of life asks for a change. But it could just be alright by correcting. Handling situations will be easy when you are a capable person. To be a capable person, correct yourself and make yourself a better person.

Peter Ferdinand Drucker was an Austrian-American management consultant, educator, and author, whose writings contributed to the philosophical and practical foundations of the modern business corporation. Drucker came up with the book, Managing Oneself a short book written by Peter Drucker in 1999 and published by Harvard Business Review. Drucker says in this book that today, in a society where most of us are knowledge workers and will have a useful working life of about 50 years, it is essential to learn to manage ourselves. In managing ourselves, Drucker mentions not changing ourselves. Drucker points out that we all have different strengths and weaknesses, and that it only makes sense to focus on growing and cultivating your strengths. Trying to fix all of your weaknesses will be a waste of time. But, we're all bad at evaluating our strengths. We're much better at knowing what we're not good at. So he suggests constantly giving yourself feedback on how you're doing.

"Don't try to change yourself, You are unlikely to succeed. Work to improve the way you perform."
-Peter F Drucker

Don't change.Improve your strengths says Peter F. Drucker. Everything is going to be good and the patches of success are going to be cleared. Just know everything about yourself and keep changing and improving the self to be the man who deserves success. Correcting yourself will be the major principle. Be flexible to know about yourself and keep correcting.

WHAT TO EXTRACT

What you extract today, Is tomorrow's reward.

Life shows us many shades of emotions, There is never an end to the surprises life gives us. Every single day, in each and every event we are supposed to face a lot of stuff emotionally and mentally. The game is all about what you extract from that particular situation. It could be a success, a failure, a heartbreak, Humour, Insult and this could just carry on with all emotions in the practical world. What we extract from each situation or circumstance today is what gets rewarded tomorrow.

Three worlds in one Life:

Numerical number Three '3' is one of the
powerful numbers. There are three worlds in every human being's life. These three worlds are equally important in their ways. Nowadays all of us are

simultaneously experiencing these three worlds every single day. The impact of these three worlds reflects so much on the only life we live. These three words are so powerful if we know how to use them. Well, life is all about how we use these three worlds. It could be positive or negative. The three worlds are as follows:

1. Fantasy world
2. Digital world
3. Authentic world

Fantasy world

In psychology, fantasy is a broad range of mental experiences, mediated by the faculty of imagination in the human brain, and marked by an expression of certain desires through vivid mental imagery. Fantasies are typically associated with scenarios that are statistically implausible or impossible in reality. The world of fantasies in everyone's life plays a crucial role without indicating the reflections of the rewards that are related to this fantasy world. This is the world inside human brains. This has no boundaries, no rules, no limitations. Your thought is the command in this magic world. This is in our imaginations, we run this world. This is our world for each of us. This is called dreaming, daydreaming, mind wandering fantasy, spontaneous thoughts, and many other names. Daydreaming is the stream of consciousness that detaches from present situations, and external tasks when attention drifts to a more personal and internal direction. This phenomenon is common in people's daily life shown by a large-scale study in which participants spend 47% of their waking time on average daydreaming. There are many types of daydreams, and there is no consistent definition among psychologists. However, the characteristic that is common to all forms of daydreaming meets the criteria for mild dissociation. Also, the impacts of different types of daydreams are not identical. While some are undisciplined and deleterious, others may be beneficial in some way.

This world is always flexible, it has no fears, no situations which are not wanted. This is the world most people often live in. Using this world there are great people who have seen success and also the ones who have made their lives much worse every time they visit this world.

This is the world everyone loves, it's a fairytale for each one of us. The world where we are supreme, we have all the authority in this world we live the life we wanted to have,

"A tool to experience repressed desires and instincts that weren't acceptable in our waking world"-Sigmund freud

In this world we live with the most beautiful people, we travel to all the beautiful places, we see ourselves in expensive cars, houses, and fashionable lifestyles with all these we create our situations, and circumstances and we live life in that world. Each one of us rules the time and lives the impossible. The most important reasons people tend to go live in this world are to get emotional relaxation, mental peace, and to fulfill physical desires. No one stops us from doing anything in this world. This world is daydreaming which is defined as imagining or fantasise. When you imagine winning the lottery and quitting your job during a boring meeting, this is an example of when you daydream. The definition of a daydream is a fantasy or series of pleasant thoughts you have when awake that helps you to escape from reality. The major emotions and subjects for which often people go live in the fantasy world are.

Love, The person we love is ours without a question in the fantasy world. No matter what, you'll just spend a great time in the fantasy world with the person you love. Love is a triumph of imagination. Daydreams in the world of fantasies were associated with increases in feelings of happiness, love, and connection, only when participants' daydreams involved people with whom they had a high, but not low, quality relationship.

Hate, your enemies will be screwed by you. not just enemies, this goes so well and satisfies your ego a lot by winning people whom you hate for a reason and with no reasons too, This quality makes this world more special.

Past, Oftenly people after dealing with a messy situation or a tough phase in their real-world they dive into the fantasy world to time travel to the past and keep recreating things in the way they wanted to. This helps in some situations and gives regret in some situations.

Future, In this world of fantasies daydreaming about the future, boosts a lot of confidence within us. The future could be a dream, a coming up task for next year, next month or it could even be the next day. People usually when they have a big day coming the night before that big day people will imagine the day as they wanted it to go. And this helps a lot mentally by reducing stress and creating a positive impact.

Fame, Majority of people always wanted to be famous, even the people who usually say I don't need fame. In this world obviously, we make ourselves famous. This world satisfies the pleasure of being popular and getting all the fame in the particular sectors or wherever we wish to.

Rich, This is all for what people dive into the fantasy world now and then. Being rich is what everyone wants to experience and this is the only place for the poor and middle class to enjoy all the riches and for the rich to experience a more lavish lifestyle. In a split second, you can be rich with whatever you want around you by just shifting to the fantasy world.

Impression, People, in general, try to impress everyone and there are very few people who don't try to impress people but even they would like people to be impressed by them. So in this fantasy world where everyone is a hero in their own world, they will always imagine or daydream that everyone around us is impressed by what we do or by our characters. And mainly people whom we always love will be impressed in this magic world.

Super-Power, most people in this world have their special superpower which they have no way to do or have in the real world. The unrealistic powers are fantasies of many young people and also few aged people. And now it's about power. The governance over people, over communities, over places and society. From middle-aged people to old aged people they wish to have power. People love to have power over many and this world makes it possible.

Character adaptation, People very often want to live a life that others are living. This is not an inspiration that people are confused about. This is different when someone wishes to live the exact life that some other person is living. People also judge or think of the incidents or reactions of some person made and if I were in that position I would have reacted differently. This is what people think. So in this fantasy world, people see themselves in someone's life and positions and create the situations or recreate the other person's situations and react according to personal opinions.

These are the main aspects of the fantasy world.

Digital world

The phrase digital world is most commonly used when defining digital fluency, and digital literacy. The digital world is the availability and use of digital tools to communicate on the Internet, digital devices, smart devices, and other technologies.

This is the second world in our lives which is in the present days playing an important role and people are spending pretty much time in this world. This world is digitalized, it could be our phones, our computers whatever. This is what shows us what is actually happening in the real world. This world has the ability to help you in the ways you want to go. It could be good or bad. And also this world has entertainment which most people spend lots and lots of time here to pass the time with instant laughter and fun.

This world is kind of tricky, this is crazy addictive for people who cannot control themselves, This world is private too, no one knows what you are doing in this world, the people you are connecting with, the knowledge you are trying to acquire, the information you are gathering, the entertainment you are seeking, the lifestyle you are wandering and the ways you are finding to the goals or tasks you want to get to. Interests of the individual are what makes this world run, it's all about what topic, what sector, and what paths, you are interested in are what you keep digging in this world. People judge easily in this world.

This digital world gives access to the real world and has the ability to showcase your life to the public and to know the lives of other people. This digital world has all the information about the real world, the history, the present events and happenings, and the future predictions. This digital world effortlessly showcases the real world, the success, the creations, the innovations all of this seems easy through this digital world. And the entertainment for relaxation which we humans need the most as the lives are most often tired and stressed so maximum crowd always seeks the entertainment and spends most of the time in this digital world.

> **"No product is made today, no person moves today, nothing is collected, analysed or communicated without some "digital technology" being an integral part of it. That, in itself, speaks to the overwhelming 'value' of digital technology."-Louis rossetto, Founder & former editor-in-chief of weird magazine**

This digital world is amazing in how it has everything in it. It could be the guide for every step to plan for the future. This has all the knowledge, information, guidance, and stories of success, and failure. Suggestions, advice, predictions and it's all about what interest we have that matters, and this world can help so much in our interests. This had the ability to connect us all around the globe and know what's happening around the globe. And the mental stress can be managed by checking out for entertainment, the confidence could be gained by the inspiration or whatever. People spending in this world most time as to say equally as in the real world. According to a survey conducted in February 2021, nearly half of the respondents stated that on average they spent five to six hours on their phone on a daily basis, not including work-related smartphone use. A further 22 percent of respondents said that they spent three to four hours on average on their phones daily. People love to spend time in this world.

Authentic world

This is the world of reality. Which is out of one's mental and emotional space. The world outside of one's physical body is an authentic world that is practical. This world is almost opposite to the other two worlds. While those first two worlds help you with instant mental relaxation and emotional stability for a while. Where this authentic world keeps destroying them now and then. In fact people use those two worlds as an escape from this authentic world.

"The real world is not easy to live in. it is rough, it is slippery."

"Without the most clear-eyed adjustments we fall and get crushed. A man must stay sober; not always, but most of the time."
-Clarence Day

This world of reality is the world of rejections, the world of failures, the world of impossibles, heartbreaks, troubles, battles, insults, breakdowns, bad lucks, tough times, unreachable opportunities, and depths of depression, unsaid words, and this could just go on. To put this simply it's like in a stormy ocean you are in a lifeboat and have to sail alone. In this tough world don't get scared by the gloomy sky and stormy ocean, be the one who is thankful for the boat you have and keep sailing concentrating on the destination. Keep going, facing the struggles, making yourself a skillful sailor every minute, overcoming the fears, getting more capable than the previous hour, and repeating the process until they make it to the shore. Finally, they will get to the dream destination and that sweetness of success is not an instant and not for a while as the first two worlds give. But in this world it's not instant, it needs a lot of struggle to achieve something and that sweetness doesn't vanish after a while it stays as long as you keep it. And it goes up or scales up as long as you take it.

"Stormy oceans make you a skillful sailor"

This authentic world is the reality, everything is tough here. Holding onto a dream is hard, and giving up on a dream is hard, choose one among those two, of course, make sure that decision adds essence to your life.

Extract from the three worlds

The three worlds are equally important in one's life to experience the pleasure of life. The first world which is the magic world, the world of fantasies and desires is really important for a dream to begin. All the success, satisfaction of life, and everything the one who has achieved began with an imagination in the first world. In the first world the dreams where you see no failures and there is no fear to dream. The freedom to dream and make it happen is important to extract from that world. The dreams to change the world, and improving the quality of living are important. Those dreams which satisfy you for a while are important. Don't lose them when you open your eyes or wake up from that world. If that desire satisfies you so much for a while how would it be if you achieve them. Hold those dreams and prepare yourself to enter the next two worlds with this desire burning in you.

> *"Hours spent daydreaming about future plans are valuable."*
> *-Seligman*

As this world has no limits and no boundaries. Dream big which your dream should have the core interest in your soul. Dream about what you love to achieve, what you love to create. The destination, the goal, and the milestones. Just make sure all that you dream and all that you imagine are something you are going to chase right after you wake up from the fantasy world. This world is the only place you have no fear of failure, so make the best use of it by dreaming of the destinations and then go on with dreaming the possibilities.

Then hold your dreams, then after the dream trip extract all those dreams into thinking. Think of the possibilities. And there you go, the second world takes charge to help you a bit here.

World two, The digital world is a tricky one. This world has a lot of good to extract if we could do it precisely. In this world, one should have limitations and boundaries. This is way different from the first world. Well, these limitations and boundaries should be set by oneself. The digital world is so addictive and contains so much unproductivity. The extraction of the quality and productivity from this digital world helps a lot in chasing the dream or whatever knowledge and information is needed. This digital world is a great advantage for this generation of living people because our elders don't have this facility to browse the world by sitting at home. This is a blessing when it is used in top quality.

Use the best of this world and this will surely give you so much knowledge, information from history, research, ebooks, articles, and every event around the world. Keep this world as quality as possible, the quality topics, quality connections, quality communities, quality events, and so on with what involves in your chase of dream or what you wanted to achieve. This world could help you by providing hints and guides on the way to the treasure of success.

These extracts from the two worlds should be applied in the authentic world. The world of reality. The dream, goal, and destination will be extracted from the fantasy world and put into thoughts. The digital world helps in finding the path to the destination, the theory, the connections, motivation, and inspirations plenty is available in the digital world which makes the destination a little clear and visible. After these extractions from the two worlds then the game begins. Execution and implementation.

"The pessimist complains about the wind, the optimist expects it to change, The realist adjusts the sail."
-William arthur ward

In this third world which is really tough, start the sail with utmost cautiousness, confidence, and determination. This will be the practical world and it gives you all the possible struggles to face. This could be sometimes more than the struggle coming across the path. But act like the one who is in the first world, the fantasy world, fearless, optimistic, powerful simply a Hero of the phase. The game-changer. Face all the struggles, overcome every critical task and sail to the destination

"It is time to face the real world, even if it is harder and painful. I'd rather fly and crash, than just snuggle and sleep."
-Chetan bhagat

Chasing your dream is a battle, this battle has an ending that is worth all the struggle. The day you reach your goal, you are the real hero of the authentic world. Do it until you honestly could say I made it.

Rejections

When I googled the word rejection, it said "the dismissing or refusing of a proposal, idea, etc". Reading this simple definition, I felt how simply it is defined and how crazily it can screw up someone to worse. Rejection could take anyone to the depths of depression and drains all their confidence. If anyone ever advises to not get hurt by rejection, then without a doubt it's the wrong one. Imagine working so much hard to reach some point, giving your best as many hours in a day as you could, sacrificing sleep, family time, and meals and sticking yourself to the work with the best levels of determination, improving yourself as much as you could and you honestly know you are giving your 100% and then getting rejected. It sucks! No matter who is beside you to support you, no matter you know you will try again, no matter you know you don't deserve that rejection but still, at that particular point, it sucks.

Rejections are common, rejections hit everyone who is trying to do something great, who is working on a great purpose. If anyone ever said I was never rejected, then that guy never was out of his comfort zone. The big dream chase always begins with stepping out of your comfort zone. Once you are out of your comfort zone then the rejections are like waves on the way. Social rejection increases anger, anxiety, depression, jealousy, and sadness. It reduces performance on difficult intellectual tasks, and can also contribute to aggression and poor impulse control,

One cannot escape rejections, so accept the rejection and extract the good from the rejection. Put that good into work again. Rejections should not make you give up. The hurt from rejection should not let you down. deal with it in a way that should boost your pace of work and keep your desire burning more and focus more on different ways and the possible changes and you will see the progress. **Stoicism** is a philosophy that says everything is possible and accepts that even then things might not go your way. That's the Stoic response to rejection. Accepting with equanimity and moving forward with virtue is what stoicism teaches.

If you feel you are unworthy or you are less capable after rejection and if you think of giving up just for getting hit by a rejection then you have to know about a person, Daniel Seddiqui, who was named by USA Today the **"Most Rejected Man in the World"**, and has gained the title of the **World's Most Ambitious Job Seeker.** Daniel Seddiqui is the most traveled person in American history and is recognized as a job-hunting expert and cultural analyst. Daniel formed Living the Map, which raises awareness of the varying cultures, careers, and environments across the country through outreach, educational endeavors, and community building. Seddiqui has failed over 40-plus consecutive job interviews, sent out 18,000 emails, and made nearly 5,000 phone calls to finally find a path he loved. Seddiqui finally achieved his ultimate vision of working 50 Jobs in 50 States. His book, 50 Jobs In 50 States: One Man's Journey of Discovery Across America, chronicles his internal and external explorations and shares riveting stories about the people he met and the lessons he learned.

In an interview of Kathy Caprino with daniel Seddiqui, we could know about Seddiqui tough journey,

Kathy Caprino: Daniel, tell us more about why you are called the "Most Rejected Person in the World?"

What happened and what prompted you to pursue a path that led to so much rejection? **Daniel Seddiqui:** Just about everything I've tried required facing an enormous amount of rejection, beginning with the entry-level job search after graduating from the University of Southern California. In the early stages of the recession, I suffered through 120 rounds of job interviews related to my economics degree. After two years, I then developed an alternative plan to pursue a career in coaching collegiate athletics and sent out 18,000 emails, only to earn a volunteer position. In light of curiosity and a desperate attempt to discover opportunities, I came up with an idea to explore the world around me by working 50 Jobs in 50 States in 50 Weeks. With no money in my name, I sought out sponsorship but had no takers. Garmin, the GPS service responded that they didn't care if I got lost. This made for the most organic job seeking, career, and cultural exploration in America. Through this undertaking, I made nearly 5,000 phone calls to land 50 unique positions, from making cheese in Wisconsin, lobster fishing in Maine, coal mining in West Virginia to making furniture with the Amish in Pennsylvania. After my journey was complete, 60 book publishers reached out to me and then turned me down. This was only the beginning of my experience with rejection, as I have learned to fight for every inch of progress. I realized that settling can be the biggest sacrifice and could miss out on something greater. That something greater came four years later.

Caprino: What was the turning point for you - the straw-breaking moment and the deep realization that this isn't the way to go about it?

Seddiqui: When I ended up homeless and had no place to turn. I failed another job interview and had to return a suit that I had just purchased for the potential job. My parents didn't think I was trying hard enough and withdrew their support. I lost my sense of purpose, something that I held at least through competing in athletics during college. No employers gave me a chance, so I had to create my destiny. I came up with this idea to learn about careers, cultures, and environments in America which gave me a newfound purpose and that would buy 50 weeks until I could figure out what to do with my life. I never would've imagined that my journey would lead to a fulfilling path in career services.

my confidence and my sense of worth went downhill fast. I thought it would be a miracle if anyone accepted me. I felt my world was crumbling all around, even from the people closest to me. In turn, this became a blessing because my courage shot through the roof, feeling that I have nothing to lose in anything I choose to do. I stopped caring what others thought and lived life for me. That's when I did 50 Jobs in 50 States and continue to pursue the most unconventional paths to make progress. I knew I was a talented individual but needed to find an outlet where I can be myself and do things differently. One final comment: After only one week at each job, I did earn 48/50 full-time job offers because I was able to show who I was, rather than tell who I was. And, I had no experience going into each position. This proves what a good attitude, being inquisitive, and demonstrating a willingness to learn can do. My advice is that settling is the biggest sacrifice, so don't miss out on something greater.

"If the world doesn't offer anything, offer something to the world."
-Daniel seddiqui

There is so much good that Siddiqui extracted from the rejections and made a way of his own. When we could extract the lessons from the rejections we can turn the result of the next attempt into a reward. Rejections help you by offering endurance, and to reevaluate or revising the plan, the execution, and the self. Rejections boost determination and a chance to change or to get better. Accepting the rejections, revising the whole process, correcting the flaws, or making everything better by holding the determination and the burning desire for achievement are the responses to a rejection.

"The greatest trap in our life is not success, popularity or power. But self-rejection."
-Henri nouwen

Rejections are the opportunities, your plan, your project, your business, your idea, your book, your story, your creation, your innovation, your product, your dream, your goal. All these are just postponed to see the steps of success if they are rejected by the world. But they are truly rejected if you reject them by yourself. To extract good from the rejections and get closer to success.

Failure

Surprisingly, every successful person out there has stated they have experienced failures and failures are important for growth and success. The Internet is filled with inspirational quotes, articles, biographies, stories, and videos about the importance of failures. There are plenty of books that tell how to deal with failures, and what to learn from failures. Well, this tells how big is the failure in the world, and what a major role it plays in everyone's life. The fear of failure, which is sometimes referred to as **Atychiphobia**, is an irrational and persistent fear of failing. Sometimes this fear might emerge in response to a specific situation. In other cases, it might be related to another mental health condition such as anxiety or depression. Failure can make you feel demoralized, helpless, hopeless, and anxious (both consciously and unconsciously) but you can fight back. According to psychology, "Failure is seen as an opportunity to learn and grow," says Los Angeles-based psychologist Crystal I. Lee. "Failure is an opportunity to be embraced, analyzed, and picked apart, rather than something to run away from."

Philosophers say failure that it is a phenomenon that arises whenever we have made some effort, or ought to have made some effort, to achieve a goal or attain a standard, but have not done so. This is typical, though not necessarily, associated with negative self-directed emotions. So failures are something that comes across when you put effort to achieve a goal or a dream, so someone who has never failed has never tried doing anything to get to a better standard of life. Failures are common in every successful life coming.

"Failure is an important part of life and critically important part of any successful life."
-Tal ben-shahar

There is a term called **Successful failure.** This term successful failure is commonly used to refer to a failure or mistake which you learn and extract the good from, so it is not a failure entirely as it has helped you progress and ensure you do not repeat the mistake again. And to correct all the flaws and make a better attempt this time.

Thomas Alva Edison is undoubtedly one of the most prolific inventors of our lifetime. He has 1,093 patents under his name, which includes the most significant, the light bulb. His light bulb invention wasn't an instant success, he failed so many times which shows the power of determination. Thomas Alva Edison tried "two thousand" different materials in search of a filament for the light bulb. When none worked satisfactorily, his assistant complained, "All our work is in vain. We have learned nothing." Edison replied very confidently, *"Oh, we have come a long way and we have learned a lot.* We now know that there are two thousand elements which we cannot use to make a good light bulb." Edison was fired from his first two jobs for being "non-productive." As an inventor, Edison made 1,000 unsuccessful attempts at inventing the light bulb. When a reporter asked, "How did it feel to fail 1,000 times?" Edison replied, *"I didn't fail 1,000 times. The light bulb was an invention with 1,000 steps."*

There is so much from failure to extract, a failure is an attempt with few flaws to be corrected and the chance to correct them. Corrections to be made and changes if needed is what all it takes to give another shot. Failure is the realisation of the wrong steps made and wrong decisions taken. It is an enlightenment for trying again better.

"Ever tried, ever failed, no matter, try again, fail again, fail better."
-Samuel beckett

There is no question of quitting or giving up on the dream with a failure, failure is the clear indication that what you did is something that doesn't work and that's a sign which says this will work in another way or another process, all you have to do is focus more and try again. Failure always takes you closer to the doors of success but never throws you away from your destination. People often confuse 'defeat' with 'failure'. Failure is a part of the process and it has a lot of positive elements to extract which would probably help you to reach the success steps in the very next attempt. Failure is defined as, **"a lack of success."** where Defeat is defined as, **"An unsuccessful ending to a struggle or contest."** So when you know failure is a common aspect or the phase of the greatest journeys, that is when you realize failure is not the end. Extract good from failure and make the best out of it to break a leg on the next try.

GIVE UP

"The only hack of winning is not admitting defeat"

Never Give Up is the phrase that means never admit defeat. Which gives a meaning of keep trying no matter what. This phrase is very powerful and mostly used by many people these days in social media, motivational videos, articles, assembly speeches, personal counsel, etc, but this phrase has a different way of being received by the people, or few people. The understanding of this phrase is not as accurate as projecting it. The successful people put this phrase into quotes and try to tell people to keep trying and at some point in time all the struggle pays off. But the understanding of this phrase needs a little more enlightenment.

This power phrase **"Never give up"** is first used as **"Never give in"** by Sir Winston Churchill in a speech. Sir Winston Leonard Spencer Churchill, was a British statesman who served as Prime Minister of the United Kingdom from 1940 to 1945, during the Second World War, and again from 1951 to 1955. Churchill was also an officer in the British army, writer, artist, and nonacademic historian. Churchill is best remembered for successfully leading Britain through World War Two. He was famous for his inspiring speeches, and for his refusal to give in, even when things were going badly. Many people consider him the greatest Briton of all time and he's almost certainly the most famous British prime minister. On October 29, 1941, Churchill visited Harrow School (a private boarding school for boys that he attended in 1888) to hear the traditional songs of the school and deliver his speech, "Never Give In." This speech was given as the United Kingdom's continued to struggle against Nazi Germany; while also receiving support from the United States in the form of war materials to aid them in World War II. in this speech, Churchill mentioned never giving in.

"Never give in. Never give in. Never, never, never, never--in nothing, great or small, large or petty--never give in, except to convictions of honour and good sense. Never yield to force. Never yield to the apparently overwhelming might of the enemy."

The power phrase started there in 1941 and it was such a motivational line and that speech is one of the greatest speeches in world history.

Never giving up doesn't always make sense or doesn't always lead you to the path of success. Not giving up on something means holding on to it. And holding onto entering a big wall hoping it the door is nothing else but foolishness. So, never giving up doesn't apply to every situation. There will be a few situations where the dreams had to be given up to see the better results and few not giving up and try harder to reach for the better results. It's all about knowing what to give up and what not to give up.

Know what to give up

In the sail toward the great dreams and goals, it's always tough because we never have a map of what's coming or what's the next step. The moves are all risky, the ways always seem narrow. The mentors, if we have any, can help us with the suggestions which could guide us a lot but not completely. In this sail of ours, we have to take the calls which we don't regret later. The calls may hurt us, make us low, and give us a bad feeling but still, those calls will be worth it in the coming times. It's all about the mindset, the stronger you can handle the feelings brain, the taller you can stand on the calls your thinking brain makes.

In world history there are many people, many companies gave up on many of their plans, ideas, and moves. Those calls made them successful people or successful companies later. It's as simple as this, when you have no way in front of you there is no good in holding onto the strong hard rock wall thinking that will make you a way if you don't give up. People have been mistaken to think that Never giving up leads to success and that giving up is the full stop of the journey to their great dream and goals.

"Know where, what and when to give up"

Both Giving up and holding onto something are part of the hardest sails to the dream. Success is never reserved for the people who don't give up and the failure doesn't hang on as the tag for someone who gives up on something. Success does come from the decisions, and those decisions always include both giving up and holding on. It's more like being practical, acting accordingly, and Making your thinking brain take charge of the feeling brain. Know where what and when to give up. No matter how hard it feels to give it up, just act on the call and give up. And if you know what, when, and where to not give up. Hold on to it no matter how much it tears you apart and hurts you. Results always flow straight from the decisions and the work. So make smart moves. The moves which may hurt you, the moves which make you feel all that you have done till the very point may just go waste but still, take the call and make the move.

Never giving up is never for ideas, plans, dreams, goals, and relations. All these are part of the foundations. And the foundations are Purpose and principles. Never give up on the purpose and the principles. And never stubbornly hold onto the ideas you were proud of, plans you were smart at, and relation you were mostly connected to when all these does not help in the progress of your sail. You can never reach your goals and dreams if you give up on the purpose and principles. Often, similarly, you cannot reach your dreams and goals if you hold onto fewer plans and situations than you should. Change the plans as many times as it takes to reach your goal or the dream, give up on every failing plan and make the better one that takes you forward. Never wish a sinking ship to float and call it Hope, and never stay in it without planning any further saying I'm not giving up. In the voyages, there should be more practicality. Every call should be made practically. Every move should result in positive progress.

According to the research by Carsten Wrosch (a professor in the Psychology department at Concordia University) and Gregory Miller (an American Internet personality and former editor and video host of the entertainment website IGN), there are dozens of studies showing that giving up can be good. And also there are a few philosophies that ask you to give up and you will be compensated by a few different certainties. All these studies and philosophies focus on the mental stress of humans and a few other aspects. But it's different when it comes to the 2-5% of people who are fascinated by the greater dreams and visions. The Set of people who are striving to achieve their goals and dreams with hard work and determination, who are trying to get the change around them. For those people, the formula for success is not 'giving up and not 'holding on'. The formula is knowing what to give up and knowing what to hold on to.

Never give up on the purpose, the destination. Don't get tricked or fooled by the emotions or any other deviations in the journey. Don't stand right before a huge wall that has blocked your way along and say you don't give up on it, you will still wait for that wall to make its way for you. Instead, make a call to change the route, and take a better way to the destination. When the focus is on the purpose, that is when you can know what, when, and where to give up or to hold on. The purpose of Thomas Edison is to invent the light bulb. He never gave up on the purpose of inventing the bulb. But Edison failed 9,999 times trying for the bulb, which says he gave up 9,999 times on different formulas, different works, different plans, and prototypes. Imagine how practical Edison was, giving up 9,999 different works and prototypes hurts so much, yet never lost the determination and never gave up on the purpose. And the result of that hard work is so fruitful.

"Our greatest weakness lies in giving up"
-Thomas A edison

The very famous company Bayerische Motoren Werke AG, commonly referred to as BMW is headquartered in Munich, Bavaria, Germany. BMW is known as a German multinational corporate manufacturer of luxury vehicles and motorcycles. But this was not the start of this great company, nothing went according to their plan or the dream. To achieve today's reputation, which is one of the vehicles that are the epitome of class, quality, and luxury, much trial and error occurred. It is amazing to know how this legend gave up on times when it didn't go in their favor and made a new path with many other back-to-back plans and took root — the ups, downs, financial troubles, slow sales, trying times, and more. BMW was founded by Franz Josef Popp, Karl Rapp, Camillo Castiglioni in 1916. Initially, it was Rapp Motorenwerke, an aircraft manufacturing firm. The initial plan of BMW was to manufacture aircraft engines. The company manufactured aircraft engines from 1916 to 1917 and BMW's first product was a straight-six aircraft engine named the BMW Illa. In 1918 however, During the war, and against the wishes of its director Franz Josef Popp, BMW placed its emphasis on aircraft engine production, the manufacturing unit of the firm was forced to stop making aircraft engines and they had no choice but to pause and hold on the manufacturing of aircraft engines, and they held it. During the war, Unbelievably BMW survived by making pots, pans, and bicycles! Due to the fact that BMW's factories were heavily bombed during the war, its remaining west German facilities were banned from producing aircraft after the war. They had no option but to give up on what they were holding onto. And they gave up. and to make another way, they switched to motorcycle production, BMW remained in business, producing motorcycle engines, farm equipment, household items, and railway brakes. The production of the company's first motorcycle, the BMW R 32, was in 1923. BMW was already making a name for itself and being linked to greatness, as this motorcycle set a world speed record that remained unbroken until 1937. It wasn't until 1928, though, that automobiles became their business, with the first car sold as a BMW being a rebadged Dixi named the BMW 3/15. This followed BMW's acquisition of the car manufacturer Automobilwerk Eisenach. In 1951, BMW was able to produce its first car since the war — a large saloon vehicle that sat comfortably for up to six. While it was designed for the luxury market, this car did not succeed. But instead, it played an important role in re-establishing BMW's reputation as a leader in the area of technology and quality. This is how BMW entered into the automobiles and made its path of success, which it is now known for. BMW resumed its car production in Bavaria in 1952 with the BMW 501 luxury saloon, and then went on to expand its range of cars in 1955. The success and pride of BMW kept on growing to date despite all the troubles, tough times, and financial crises.

BMW never followed the phrase NEVER GIVE UP, or it never just kept on GIVING UP. At times no matter how hard it was for them they still gave up on their dream and goals, they survived by making pans, pots, and households for a few days. They came back into the market again and again with something more productive and innovative. They earlier failed in their car too. But BMW never seems to give up on its principles and purpose. They were always known for quality and technology. They set records in speed that were held by them for decades. They made their way to their destination by holding onto a few, giving up on unnecessary, and surviving tough times.

At times Giving up on something which we dreamt of for days and nights and working our ass off to get it into reality and make it happen breaks us to disappointment. and that is a different kind of low. But at that very point in time or the situation, giving up is the step that should be taken. And at times Holding onto something which is tearing apart and does not seem to fall back into place is so tough because it kind of gives a feeling that holding it doesn't make any sense and the longer you hold onto that the more severe it hurts but that stuff is worth it. *Juice is always worth the squeeze.* And sometimes between this giving up and holding onto there is survival. This part is where most dreams were killed, most of the sails being failed. Well, all it takes to survive is the hunger to achieve and the primary focus on the purpose of the journey.

"Be Savvy enough to Give up, And Canny enough to hold on."

EITHER - OR

The world runs by the concept of Either-Or but most people choose the concept of Neither - Nor. Both of these concepts are quite opposite ways which show completely opposite mindsets of people who follow what. Most successful people in the world always focus on either - or. And the majority of the crowd who always makes excuses set themselves for neither - nor. When I mentioned these two as concepts this doesn't mean the behavior of an individual but it is the offering from many aspects in the world for which there are only two possibilities and what we choose among those two will make us a person with a vision or a person with excuses. To explain it understandably we will choose a topic, profit, and loss.

Either Profit or loss

Everything around us is profit and loss, most successful people handle it as either profit or loss, and that is when they can accept their profits and losses and learn from them. And the unsuccessful people handle it Neither profit nor loss. That's when they get satisfied on that parallel line and there is no scope for growth.

In the journey or the sail to achieve the greatest dreams and goals, In every situation, every struggle, every failure, every milestone, every achievement, and from every small step there is profit and loss, and that should be handled as Either profit or loss. There will either be profit in the particular step or loss in the particular situation, there can never be both which is neither profit nor loss in any kind of situation. This is something I followed and found the results helped me to grow from the failures and also the **illusion of success.** When I was in my early business with my startup, I figured my profit and loss as Either profit or loss.

End of the week or the month when my team closes all the monthly and weekly calculations and gets the final results, There are times We made a profit in money and there are times we made a loss. So when we make good money that doesn't count in profit all the time, our mistakes matter, our wrong steps all over the month count too, based on all those we may make a good amount of money but we may lose a couple of customers and end of the day that goes into Loss. and pretty often when we made good money and we made no mistakes it goes into profit obviously. Then in the days, we lost money of course that counts as a Loss, but not always. There are days we learned a lot by losing money, the mistakes are so damn worthy that my team and I were glad to learn that lesson for a certain amount of money, or we are just thankful we learned the lesson from that particular mistake in an early stage or if its a little late we would have lost more money, efforts, and customers too. In that case, losing money and sales for a month is still a profit for us. And of course, the loss of money without any lessons learned is into the category of loss. And in between these two, there are times when we didn't make any money and didn't lose any money too, but even then it's neither or nor, the mission ours is to make a certain amount of money but we fail and that, of course, counts into a loss.

Money, rank, appreciation, rewards, recognition, bonus, penalties, notices, all these are part of your profit and loss but never alone your profit or loss. So profit and loss never depend on a single outcome but it includes a lot more aspects individually. So the concept of either or in calculating profit or loss is something very useful for growth, realization, and every next step in life and career.

Some people see profit and loss in general when they didn't make good money that's not profitable for them when they made a good amount that's profit when they lost money that's a loss, when they don't lose any money and don't make any good money that is neither profit nor loss. This mindset is a common mindset that is in general by the majority of the population. When you are chasing a big dream the very first step is to separate yourself from the crowd, which means the way of thinking, way of earning, way of spending, way of reading, talking, listening, and every small thing. There is always either or in everything but there should never be neither nor. There is self-limiting in neither nor, there is growth in either or.

Either 1 or 0

The concept of winning should also be in a different vision, There comes the concept of either-or again. It's always 1 or 0, there is no 2nd place, 3rd place, and 10th place. Winning is the 1st place, and the rest of everything is not winning. 2nd place also is not winning and because it's Either 1 or 0, 2nd place also goes to 0.

Winning is different from the vision of the world and from individually within ourselves. In the journey to the dreams and the goals, there should never be a race with another person or any other except you alone. It goes like this, you set a target in every small to large time frame, if you achieve it then you win, if you are even just an inch away from achieving it, you lose. In a test, if your target is to score 95 out of 100, only 95 and above makes you a winner no matter how many people scored 98 and 99. And even 94.5 makes you a loser because you didn't reach your target and no matter no one could score 94.5 except you. So it's about what the target you set for yourself and not with others. Winning is so sweet that when you achieve your target and everyone around you may or may not notice but you know that you achieved the target that you were working hard on, and what you've learned. There are no 2nd and 3rd places, the mindset should be Either 1 or 0. The target, the goal which you set for the milestones should be higher, as high as if anyone reached that target it would be the 1st place. When you are concentrating on the 2nd and 3rd position is something which you've already admitted defeat from 1st place and this kind of mindset is no good to give another try also, cause when you accept making in 2nd or 3rd position or even 10th position is a win too then that's a satisfactory mindset. This mindset can never make you a real winner.

"second place is just the first loser"
-Dale Earnhardt

Dale Earnhardt,

Ralph Dale Earnhardt Sr. (April 29, 1951 - February 18, 2001) was an American professional stock car driver and team owner, who raced from 1975 to 2001 in the former NASCAR Winston Cup Series (now called the NASCAR car series), most notably driving the No. 3 Chevrolet for Richard Childress Racing. He began his career in 1975 in the world of 600. Earnhardt won a total of 76 Winston Cup races throughout his 26-year career, including four Winston 500s (1990, 1994, 1999, and 2000) and the 1998 Daytona 500. He is the only driver in NASCAR history to score at least one win in 4 different and consecutive decades (scoring his first career win in 1979, 38 wins in the 1980s, 35 wins in the 1990s, & scoring his final two career wins in 2000). He also earned seven Winston Cup championships, a record held by Richard Petty and Jimmie Johnson. Although he is tied for most championships, he is the only driver in NASCAR history to win seven championships under one single points system, and he is also the only driver in NASCAR history to finish either 1st or 2nd in the standings ten times under one single points system. His aggressive driving style earned him the nicknames "The Intimidator", "The Man in Black", and "Ironhead". He is regarded as one of the greatest drivers, and by many NASCAR fans, the greatest driver in NASCAR history.

**"The winner ain't the one with the fastest car, it's the one who refuses to lose."
-Dale earnhardt**

On February 18, 2001, Earnhardt died in a sudden last-lap crash during the Dayton 500 due to a basilar skull fracture, an event that is regarded in the racing industry as being a crucial moment in improving safety in all aspects of car racing, especially NASCAR. Earnhardt has been inducted into numerous halls of fame, including the NASCAR hall of fame inaugural class in 2010.

In this amazing career of Dale Earnhardt, there is another important record that should be noticed: the number of second-place finishings. Dale Earnhardt famously once said, **"second place is just the first loser."** Ironically, if this rings true, Earnhardt was the first loser 70 times in his illustrious, seven-championship career. Only four drivers have tallied more career second-place finishes than this Intimidator. Finishing in 2nd place 70 times and still having a famous saying of Second place is just the first loser says the acceptance and mindset of a true winner. He would have never been so proud of finishing in second place, and that's what made him finish in 1st in later times.

Champions are built differently, the mindsets are different, the way they take success is different, the way they accept failure is different and the way they grind is different. Success starts from the mindset of every dreamer. The dream begins and the second thing which should happen is to build a mindset. The growth mindset. And this is the concept of an either-or mindset which will help you in the tough sails.

Conclusion

Journey to success is
Never less than 'Tough'

Brian Tracy is a Canadian-American motivational public speaker and self-development author. He said this in one of his speeches, The first million is hard, but the second million is inevitable. It's not becoming a millionaire that's important, it's the person that you must become in order to become a millionaire, you have to become a completely different person. You have to develop the character beyond 99% of people in the world, you have to develop honesty and discipline and quality relationships and the ability to work and set priorities and all kinds of stuff. Because without that nothing is possible.

From a particular type of person to a completely different person is what success makes you. Through all the trenches, failures, rejections, lessons, and survivals the person you will become is what success is. The way you think brings all the differences, there come the situations when to make the tough calls, and all the decisions are very important in the journey. Fight every little battle as if it is your last one. Raise from the trenches, learn from the failures and keep the desire burning inside you. Have the belief and make yourself a person whom you can trust and pursue everything you dream of. Every bad day passes, every tough situation ends, and no favor could be on your side all the time. Still, the consistency of your hard work takes you to shore. Be clear about every little happening, process, and progress. Build a lifestyle of productivity and quality. In the sail to your dream, Thunder shouldn't scare you, storms shouldn't stop you. Make yourself a skillful and smart sailor. The top of every floor is the bottom of another, learning never stops, and everything you learn in the journey rewards you with massive success.

For everyone who is dreaming big, let consistency and commitment be your constant. And everything you work for will find its way sooner or later. Jack Ma said his life's principle is: Today is hard, tomorrow will be worse, but the day after tomorrow will be sunshine. Most people give up tomorrow evening. So never stop trying and fighting. If it is in your mind then for sure you can get it in real life. Wishing this book helps you in the hardest puzzled situations of your sail and guides you with the topics and real inspirations included here.

"The person who doesn't have it,
knows the value of it.
Who earns it, knows the worth of it."

Be thankful for every small thing you have today, begin with whatever you have with you. Rich never wastes anything, Time too. Cause they know the worth of it. Talk to yourself and start within yourself, inside control and focus are what get you all your energy outside.

Start to sail, Sail the storm.
-Daniel abhishikth

When you come out of the storm,
you won't be the same person who walked in.
~ Haruki Murakami

Thank you for reading.
Wishing everything you dream and working hard for will find its way to you.
By Daniel Abhishikth B

www.ingramcontent.com/pod-product-compliance
Lightning Source LLC
Chambersburg PA
CBHW061341160726
47995CB00001B/125